St. Louis Community College

Forest Park
Florissant Valley
Meramec

Instructional Resources
St. Louis, Missouri

BLACKS IN THE NEW WORLD

August Meier, Series Editor

A list of books in the series Blacks in the New World
appears at the end of this book.

Charles Richard Drew

Charles Richard Drew

The Man and the Myth

Charles E. Wynes

University of Illinois Press
Urbana and Chicago

Library of Congress Cataloging-in-Publication Data

Wynes, Charles E.
    Charles Richard Drew : the man and the myth / Charles E. Wynes.
    p. cm.—(Blacks in the New World)
Bibliography: p.
Includes index.
ISBN 0-252-01551-7
1. Drew, Charles Richard, 1904–1950.   2. Physicians—United
    States—Biography.   3. Afro-American physicians—Biography.
I. Title.   II. Series.
R154.D75W96 1988
610'.92'4—dc19
[B]   88-4738
                                               CIP

*For the family, the friends, and
the former students and residents of*
Charles Richard Drew, M.D. (1904–50)

Contents

It must be borne in mind that my design is not to write histories but lives. And the most glorious exploits do not always furnish us with the clearest indications of virtue or vice in men; sometimes a matter of less moment, an expression or a jest, informs us better of their characters and inclinations than sieges, the greatest armaments, or the bloodiest battles. Therefore, as portrait-painters are more exact in the lines and features of the face, in which the character is seen, than in the other parts of the body, so I must be allowed to give my more particular attention to the marks and indications of the souls of men. . . .

—Plutarch, *Lives of Nine Illustrious Greeks and Romans*

Preface

This study, which is really more of a biographical interpretation than a traditional biography, was written primarily for the general reading public, especially those who either have heard of the role Charles Richard Drew played in the development of blood plasma transfusions or of the controversy surrounding his death, or both. Therefore, deliberately I have kept "scholarly impedimenta" to a minimum. For instance, only direct quotations have been annotated. All other documentation appears in the form of general notes which follow the numbered notes for each chapter. In addition, however, a bibliography in the form of an essay is included. Finally, in both style and content, I have sought to capture the person and the personality of Charles R. Drew rather than to write a "definitive" and detailed life, or life and times, of the subject.

The Charles R. Drew who emerges from these pages probably does not exactly match the man remembered by any one person who knew him, whether family member, friend, colleague, or former student. Rather, here is the composite "Charlie" Drew, or "Big Red," whom they all knew (or at least knew a part of) and—the Charles Drew who was revealed only in his most intimate correspondence. The final result, or picture, that emerges is one that captures Charles R. Drew from many angles or perspectives as seen by this, his first, biographer—first except for those who (with good, or at least well-intentioned, reasons) have written juvenile or fictional biographies of this remarkable American.

University of Georgia, 1988   Charles E. Wynes

Acknowledgments

For this book I am indebted to many persons and institutions. First and foremost, I am indebted to Mrs. Charles Richard Drew, Sr., the widow of Dr. Drew, and to their daughter Bebe Roberta (Mrs. Kline A. Price) for permission to use the personal papers of Dr. Drew in the Moorland-Spingarn Research Center at Howard University. Without access to those papers this study would have been the story of a very great medical scientist and physician only, while now it is that of diarist, humanist, and even philosopher as well.

On another plane, I am indebted beyond measure to Joseph L. Drew, Dr. Drew's brother, who has helped me in so many ways. He, together with his wife, Grace (Ridgeley) Drew, spent the better part of a day talking with me and answering questions about the man whom some called "Big Red." While visiting with them in their home in Arlington, Virginia, I was even shown the room where Charlie slept as a boy. And from time to time, over the years this biography was in the making, Joseph Drew has filled in informational gaps, corrected me on factual matters, identified photographs, and, in the process, become a warm and respected friend, as has Grace, his wife.

Among the Drew family, I am also indebted, for both oral and written reminiscences, to Dr. Drew's sister Nora (Mrs. Francis Gregory) who, one hot summer afternoon, took me into her home, where Mr. and Mrs. Joseph Drew had brought me, and talked about Charlie as if he had just left the room.

Talking about Charlie can become a warm and fascinating contagion, as I learned myself while talking with those who had known Drew—as fellow medical student, as colleague, as teacher, and, above all, as friend. Each of those persons told me at least something that I had heard from no other, while all of them repeated or corroborated certain stories, or described the same traits of character in Dr. Drew, that I had heard about over and over. In so doing, they made for the telling of a more accurate story here, as well as adding their own unique perspective.

Among those persons who knew Drew were three lifelong friends and colleagues at Howard University and Freedmen's Hospital: Dr. W. Montague Cobb, Dr. Burke Syphax, and Dr. Samuel L. Bullock. Dr. Cobb is a walking encyclopedia, while Dr. Syphax, an imposing and forceful man, was especially helpful in cutting through myth, rumor, and innuendo. Dr. Bullock, friendly, frank, and outgoing, made a delightful interviewee.

Equally helpful, and still adoring, were two of Drew's former surgical residents, Dr. Jack White, now retired Chief of Cancer Research at Howard University, and Dr. Asa G. Yancey, Associate Dean, Emeritus, of the medical school at Emory University and Medical Director at Grady Memorial Hospital in Atlanta. Dr. White is a born storyteller and a vivid one, too, while Dr. Yancey repeatedly has gone out of his way to be extra helpful to me.

Yet another contemporary and friend of Drew's, who shared with me recollections of their medical school days at McGill University, was Dr. Richard B. Dunn, a retired gynecologist in Greensboro, North Carolina.

Other medical people who were eager to assist me and did, were Professors Emeriti Edward H. Bensley and Reginald A. Wilson at McGill University.

Unique among my medical sources, however, was Dr. Charles E. Kernodle, Jr., one of the three physicians who treated Drew following his fatal accident. Dr. Kernodle phoned me when he learned that I was working on the biography. There then followed frequent correspondence which culminated in a visit with Dr. Kernodle in Burlington, North Carolina. With him I visited the site of the accident, and together we stood on the spot in the onetime emergency room of the old Alamance County General Hospital building where Charles R. Drew died. Dr. Kernodle, a surgeon, like Drew, is the kind of physician whom Drew himself might have called a doctor's doctor.

In the Moorland-Spingarn Research Center at Howard University, where the Drew papers are located, I found willing, able, and enthusiastic help from the entire staff. Karen Jefferson, Wilda Logan-Willis, Esme Bhan, and Paul Coates, especially, made my stay there a rewarding and delightful one.

And while I was in Washington, D.C., Rudolf A. Clemen and Fern Bowser of the American Red Cross National Headquarters unstintingly and ably assisted me in what I came to call my "blood research."

From the headquarters of the American Medical Association in Chicago, James McDonald made me feel almost guilty for some of the harsh things that I felt compelled to write about the AMA and its policy regarding black membership. Holding back nothing, Mr. McDonald freely revealed to me the not very admirable record of the AMA in that area. He also provided reams of copied records, nearly all of them condemnatory—and all gratis.

At my own university, the University of Georgia, the late Robert C. Anderson, Vice-President for Research, was ever-generous with travel funds, but, more than that, he was a fellow humanist who understood what I was trying to do, appreciated it, and then provided me with the wherewithal to do it. He was a true patron. Also at the University of Georgia, I am indebted to Kathy Coley, who typed and retyped the manuscript. Sensitive and perceptive, she was indeed an editor to me.

At the Rockefeller Archive Center, North Tarrytown, New York, I am indebted to Darwin Stapleton, Melissa Smith, and Thomas Rosenbaum. All three are dedicated archivists, and they made me feel at home in the Rockefeller mansion that houses the center.

About the country, here and there, there are others to whom I am indebted, among them: Max M. Way of the Alamance County Historic Properties Commission, Graham, North Carolina, for photographs of the site of the Drew automobile accident and the historic marker now there in Drew's honor; Robert Michel, Archivist, McGill University; John Hope Franklin, Professor Emeritus, Duke University; George Stevenson of the North Carolina State Archives in Raleigh; Richard T. Howerton III, Administrator, Alamance County Hospital; Tom Thompson, Director of Alumni Relations, McGill University; and Joanne C. Dougherty, Assistant Archivist, Amherst College.

To August Meier of Kent State University, General Editor of the series of which this book is a part, I am indebted for his longtime example, through his own publications, in the area of black history. For more than a quarter of a century our paths have crossed from time to time, and, while I knew "Augie" to be a fine scholar, I now know him to be a fine editor as well. Sometimes he let me "win a few," where I felt strongly about my views and interpretations, but mostly I simply deferred to what I felt was his good, even better, judgment.

At the University of Illinois Press, I am indebted to Richard L. Wentworth, Director, and to all his fine staff, especially Beth Bower, my editor. She pruned, she sharpened, and always she improved—including even that prose of which I was proudest, while yet leaving it clearly my own. As such, she was artist, not just editor.

Finally, but by no means least, there is Carolyn Wynes, my wife, to whom I am indebted for far more than the usual "devotion, support, forbearance, etc." She was helpmate and research associate as, day after day, we worked our way through the personal papers of Charles R. Drew at Howard University. Indeed, it was she who first recognized the inestimable value of Drew's soul-revealing letters to his wife, Lenore, found here in chapters 6 and 11. Then, too, she even transcribed all the letters in shorthand, since at that time photocopying of them was not permitted.

To all of the above, my friends, I am deeply indebted.

Introduction

It was around 2:15 in the morning on Saturday, April 1, 1950, while Washington, D.C., still slept, that four black physicians—Drs. Samuel L. Bullock, Charles R. Drew, John R. Ford, and Walter R. Johnson—departed from northwest Washington in a 1949 black four-door Buick Roadmaster belonging to Bullock. Jovial and relaxed, all four were looking forward to a leisurely trip south, with a stopover in Atlanta, to Tuskegee, Alabama. There they were to participate in an annual free clinic for Deep South blacks sponsored by the John A. Andrew Memorial Hospital (named for Andrew, abolitionist and Civil War governor of Massachusetts, and built with funds contributed by his daughter, Elizabeth Andrew Mason, in 1912). The patients, who were mostly rural and generally poor, came from all over the region, seeking diagnosis and treatment; the staff, made up of medical professors and clinicians, both black and white, came from all over the nation to examine and treat them, seeking to learn in the process.

Originally Bullock and Drew had intended to fly to Alabama (Drew's wife begged him to take the train), but they later decided to drive so that Ford and Johnson could accompany them. Since the clinic was not scheduled to begin until Monday, April 3, they had the entire weekend to make the trip.

Bullock was driving as they left Washington, while Drew, who was to relieve him, rested. Drew's busy schedule the previous day had included performing operations most of the day at Freedmen's

1

Hospital, then attending a Howard University student council meeting that evening. In all, he had caught only about two hours of sleep.

Crossing the Fourteenth Street Bridge over the Potomac River, the four headed south on U.S. Route 1 through the warm and greening Virginia countryside. At Petersburg, south of Richmond, Drew took the wheel, and, about a hundred miles farther on, just before reaching the Virginia–North Carolina line (as Johnson recalled), they made a brief rest stop. Refreshed, they got back into the car, with Drew still driving. Bullock was seated beside him, with Ford in the back behind Drew, and Johnson behind Bullock. The passengers dozed off. Then, at about 7:50 A.M. on a straight stretch of North Carolina State Route 49, two miles north of the town Haw River, Bullock recalled being awakened as the wheels of the car dropped off the right shoulder of the road.

"Hey, Charlie!" he called out to Drew, who was apparently dozing. Awakening, Drew cut the wheels sharply to the left, taking the car completely across the road into a plowed field, where it turned over three times. Drew was partly thrown from the car, which rolled over him, while Ford (seated behind him) was thrown clear.

Johnson awakened, unhurt, to find himself still sitting in the same position (in the back to the right). The car was right side up, but about thirty yards from the road, and it faced south, the way they had been traveling. Having no idea what had happened, Johnson thought he was all alone, until he discovered Bullock partially wedged under the dashboard. Johnson set about freeing Bullock, who had sustained only cuts on one hand. Ford was sitting upright on the ground some forty feet from the car, where he had been thrown. His left arm apparently was broken and he had lacerations on his legs, but otherwise he was not seriously hurt. Drew was partly in the car and partly out of it, with his right foot caught under the brake pedal. He was alive, but obviously in shock, with a nearly severed left leg and internal injuries (as then undetermined), both sustained when the car rolled over him.

There, in that plowed field, the life of Charles R. Drew rapidly was ebbing away. He who had done so much to save the lives of others was now himself beyond the help of medical science.

In just under forty-six years Drew had become a truly legendary figure—as athlete, as research scientist, and as surgeon, but perhaps most of all, as a trainer and teacher of other black surgeons. So legendary had he become that from time to time, both during his life and after it, the legend became bigger than the man, as often happens in the case of truly exceptional people. Thus it is not easy to separate the legendary achievements of Charles R. Drew from the fabricated legends that tenaciously cling to his memory. Similarly, it is difficult to place those achievements in proper perspective, though Drew himself never had any trouble naming what he considered to be his greatest achievement—and it was not the one the public chose. He chose his role as teacher and trainer of other black surgeons, while the public chose his blood plasma research.

After his death, the legends continued to grow, clouding the truth even more, but the one surrounding the circumstances of his death in particular would come to be the greatest legend of them all.

The road to all these legends passed through many places before it reached that North Carolina field on a cruelly ironic April Fools' Day: the "Foggy Bottom" area of Washington, D.C., where Drew's life began; Dunbar High School, Amherst College, McGill University Medical School, Columbia-Presbyterian Hospital, and Columbia University, where the promise of his true talent first appeared and then developed; and then New York and Washington, D.C., the respective sites of Drew's work in blood plasma and his labors as a surgeon and trainer of surgeons, where his talent came to flower.

What follows is the story, and the legend, of the life of Charles Richard Drew. His family and his friends called him "Charlie." His students and his younger colleagues (just among themselves) called him "Big Red."

NOTES

Baltimore Afro-American, April 4, 1950; *Burlington Times-News,* April 1, 1950, and April 1, 1980; Hamilton Bims, "Charles Drew's 'Other' Medical Revolution," *Ebony,* 30 (Feb., 1974): 88–96; John R. Ford to Claude H. Organ, January 30, 1980, Charles Richard Drew Papers, Moorland-Spingarn Research Center, Howard University (hereinafter cited as CRD Papers); *Greensboro Daily News and Record,* July 11, 1982; John

R. Ford to Devra M. Breslow, March 12, 1971 (copy in possession of the author); W. Montague Cobb to Edward V. Sparer, February 11, 1980, CRD Papers; interview with Dr. Samuel L. Bullock; *Pittsburgh Courier,* April 1, 1950.

1

Roots

Charles Richard Drew first saw the light of day at 1806 E Street, NW, Washington, D.C., in a rambling, three-story, sixteen-room house that stood on the corner where the United States Department of the Interior Building now stands. The day was June 3, 1904, and the house was that of his maternal grandparents, Joseph and Emma (Mann) Burrell. His mother, Nora Rosella Drew, had wanted to be with her own mother when the baby was born, and since the older woman could not leave the rest of her family, Nora went home to her, moving from 821 Twenty-first Street, NW, the home of her in-laws. Nora and her husband, Richard, had been living there since their marriage on June 24, 1903. Although Nora's mother, Emma, was a midwife, the baby was ushered into the world by Dr. Charles Marshall, the family physician. But, of course, it was not for the doctor that he was named; instead, it was for his paternal uncle, Charles Drew.

The huge house where Charlie, as they called him, was born, was a regular birthing center for both the Drews and the Burrells—most of them were born there. At one time, according to the census of 1910, there were eighteen persons living there: Joseph and Emma Burrell, eight of their children, two sons-in-law, three grandchildren, two brothers-in-law, and one sister-in-law! Mrs. Nora (Drew) Gregory, one of Charlie's sisters, remembers it as a happy place, one with "a feeling of family."[1]

The birthplace of Charlie was located in a part of Washington known as "Foggy Bottom"—so named because of the frequent evening and early morning fogs that arose from the Potomac River. It was not, as some overly imaginative writers would have it, an area of unpainted, ramshackle houses set on posts along unpaved and unlighted streets. Foggy Bottom was middle-class America, and it was an interracial community, with pockets of Irish, Negroes, Italians, and even French. Most of the houses were two-story red brick, with both front and backyards, which sometimes were enclosed by iron fences. There was a large park across the street with two swimming pools, one for Negroes and one for whites, while on the south side of the Washington Monument there was the Sylvan Theater, which provided summer entertainment. There were also two white elementary schools, and two for Negroes.

Richard and Nora, together with the infant Charlie, continued to live with Richard's parents at 821 Twenty-first Street, NW, until 1905, when they all moved three blocks to No. 1149. Then in 1908, when Grandmother Martha Drew died, the family separated. Richard and Nora and their two children, Charlie and Elsie (born on August 16, 1906), moved back into the huge, old house at 1806 E Street. There, two more little Drews were born—another boy, Joseph L., on July 20, 1909, and a second girl, Nora, on May 10, 1913.

In 1914, with their family almost complete, Richard and Nora and their four children moved a few doors down to No. 1826. Finally, in October 1920, they moved across the Potomac River into Virginia to 2505 First Street, Arlington, where their fifth and last child, Eva, was born on December 12, 1921. But by then only four children remained, for earlier, on May 22, 1920, Elsie, their first daughter, had died of tuberculosis.

The Arlington home, a comfortable two-story frame house with a yard all around, now became the Drew homestead. Today it is still lived in by Drews: Richard and Nora's second son, Joseph L., and his wife, Grace (Ridgeley) Drew live there. It also bears a plaque indicating that it is on the National Register of Historic Places.

The parents of Charles R. Drew, who provided these comfortable middle-class surroundings for their children, were themselves achievers. Nora was a graduate of Howard University who made her children her career and never worked outside the home. Richard had less formal education than his wife, since economic necessity had led him to drop out of high school before he finished. Like his father before him, he was a carpet-layer by trade, and he worked for the Moses Furniture Company, which mostly served the needs of the area's hotels and other public facilities. A union member, he was financial secretary of Local 85 of the Carpet, Linoleum, and Soft Tile-Layers Union. He was also the local's only Negro member. Red-haired and freckled, with a moustache he grew to cover a badly cut lip gained in a boxing match (he engaged in boxing for sport), Richard was a gregarious and outgoing man. He also played both the piano and the guitar, and sang in a barbershop quartet as well as in the choir of the Nineteenth Street Baptist Church, a favorite of many of the Washington, D.C., black elite.

However, it was from both his parents that Charlie learned to love music, since his mother also sang. Later he "tootled" on the saxophone and "plinked" at the piano. His repertoire consisted of only two tunes—one, which his friends called "Drew's Blues," and another, which nobody seems to remember the name of.

It is not easy to trace Drew's ancestry, on either side, beyond a few generations. His father, Richard, born in 1878 in Washington, was the son of Richard Thomas, Sr. (1852–1915), and Martha (Taylor) Drew (1859–1908). Richard Thomas, Sr., Drew's grandfather, came to Washington sometime in the 1870s from Charlottesville, Virginia, while his grandmother, Martha Taylor, came from Winchester, Virginia. Drew's great-grandfather, Thomas Drew (1828–68 or 1870), was a barber and a free man in Charlottesville, while his great-grandmother, Elizabeth (last name unknown), reportedly was part Indian. Beyond that point, Drew's paternal ancestry is too sketchy to trace meaningfully.

On the maternal side, Drew's mother, Nora (1880–1962), was the daughter of Emma (Mann) Burrell (1859–1926), and the granddaughter of Robert and Margaret (Freeman) Mann (dates?) of Upperville, Virginia. Margaret was white. Nora's father, Joseph, was born in Georgetown, District of Columbia, and that is all that is known about his beginnings. Further back than that, Drew's maternal ancestry is even sketchier than his paternal one.

Both the Drews and the Burrells were racially categorized as Negro Americans—by the Census Bureau, by the white world about them, and perhaps by themselves as well. But in fact they were just Americans of mixed ancestry—part Negro, part English, part Scot, and part Indian. Where the Drews and the Burrells came from was not nearly so important as who they were and what they strove to become. Mrs. Nora Gregory recalled that the Drew children were *expected* to do their best. And they did.

If the Foggy Bottom of the early 1900s was a good environment in which to grow up (and it was), the household of Richard and Nora Drew, with its warmth and supportiveness, provided an atmosphere that was almost nineteenth-century idyllic. The church played a large role in the lives of all the Drews, and at home the family joined in kneeling prayer and Bible reading on Sunday mornings, led by Charlie's father. There were also books in the house—including an encyclopedia, volumes of Shakespeare, the *Classic Myths,* books on opera, and numerous novels, among others—and they were read. Similarly, the larger world of Washington outside Foggy Bottom was not unfamiliar to the growing children since their father took them about the city, introducing them to its monuments, public buildings, and museums. Despite Washington's segregation, the Drews lived a life that was somehow insulated from the worst affronts of that system. Certainly there was no bitterness, Mrs. Nora Gregory recalled, as she looked back upon that world of some sixty years ago.

Also, in the Drew home the children were not just children. They were, instead, functioning members of the household, each with his or her own responsibilities for cleaning, setting the table, washing the dishes, and so on. It was thus no wonder that Charlie could, years later, approach surgical training already knowing how to "sew." He had learned at home, because it was expected of him when it came to taking care of his own clothes.

Yet as long as he lived there was never any doubt about who was head of the household, and it was Drew, senior. Nora, his wife, knew it, and she did not let her children forget what they owed their father, as years later she told them: "Don't you ever forget that you were cared for and educated by your father on his knees," referring to how he earned the family's livelihood—on his knees, laying carpet. Mrs. Nora Gregory remembered how, when Charlie was at Amherst College and at McGill University Medical School, their father would cash his check and send Charlie a money order before he brought the rest home for himself, his wife, and the other children. Charlie would always immediately write back: "I received the blue [meaning the blue money order]. Thank you." [2]

Some have thought that Charlie, because he was the first son and the oldest child, was the favorite of his parents. He was not, for there were no favorites. Years later, after Charlie had achieved a measure of fame as athlete, research scientist, and surgeon, when someone would ask Nora (as they often did), "How is your son?," meaning Charlie, she would reply: "Which one? I have four"— which was her way of saying that she accorded to her two sons-in-law the same status she did to her two natural sons. [3] One does not easily forget such a mother. On the other hand, deferential as she was to her husband when he was alive, when he died in 1935 after all the children but Eva were grown, there was never any doubt about who then headed the Drew clan—it was she, and not Charlie, as sometimes has been said.

It was thus a comfortable and, economically speaking, reasonably secure home in which to grow up, with all family members having a productive role to fill. Still, Charlie, being the oldest child, perhaps chafed more than the others for a greater measure of independence—his own money, for instance—especially as he approached his teens. But then, too, it was expected in that day that city boys (and, less frequently, city girls) should, by that age, have some kind of job. (Of course, on the farm there was rarely any choice between working and not working for either sex, and no pay was expected for the work and none forthcoming, except maybe a dollar here and a dollar there—pocket change for a Saturday trip to town.)

Charlie, at age twelve, in the old "American-as-apple-pie" tradition, became a paperboy, hawking the *Washington Times and Herald* and the *Evening Star* in the afternoons from a stand at the corner of Eighteenth and E Streets. Within a year, though, Charlie was no longer just a paperboy—he was a "newspaper entrepreneur," with six other boys working for him. Later, especially after the family moved to Arlington, Virginia, Charlie worked at playgrounds after school. There was also work on construction jobs.

School, however, came first—his parents never let him forget that—and though Charlie was a slow starter academically, there was never any doubt that he had the intellectual wherewithal to do just about anything he set his mind to. But for a long time, his goal was athletics. By age eight, while he was still a student at Stevens Elementary School (named for the Vermont-born abolitionist and Radical congressman from Pennsylvania, Thaddeus Stevens), Charlie was already engaging in competitive swimming meets. Football, basketball, and track would come in turn; he was good, even exceptional, at them all.

In the spring of 1918, Charlie finished Stevens Elementary School, and after a summer devoted largely to athletics—and newspapers, of course—he entered Dunbar High School that fall. Named in honor of the Negro poet Paul Laurence Dunbar, Dunbar High was probably the best segregated high school in the nation; indeed, it was also one of the best high schools anywhere, for anybody. Dunbar was for the academically elite, but, fortunately, it was not unique, for at other places in the South there were Dunbar equivalents. However, unlike the school in Washington, they were often private and sometimes affiliated with a black college. According to David L. Lewis, author of *District of Columbia: A Bicentennial History* (1976), "Where such schools were public, white indifference or guilt allowed them to thrive quietly. Where private, the black bourgeoisie heroically assumed the burden." Lewis says that at Dunbar "white indifference and guilt and black elitism operated in collusion." There, prominent black families, like the Bruces, the Cobbs, the Syphaxes, the Wormleys, and the Weavers, "were resolved to make the school their special, exclusive domain, a crucible for the formation of unpoor, well-bred, and generally [but by no means always] light-skinned clients."[4] There was no better public college preparatory school in the nation's capital, for either race.

At Dunbar no concessions were made to "progressivism," "relevance," "cultural deprivation," or "vocationalism," with Latin always, and Greek for a while, a part of the curriculum. Its principals frequently were educated at Harvard, Oberlin, Amherst, and Dartmouth, while its teachers held solid academic degrees, not "education" degrees. It was small wonder, then, that from all over the city, without regard to school zones, black students seeking a first-class secondary education came to Dunbar. And from nearby Maryland and Virginia communities—where either no Negro high schools existed, or the ones that did were inferior—came Negro students who simply gave the address of relatives or friends who lived in the District of Columbia. Among these students were the Drews from Arlington.

Dunbar simply "was left alone to operate as a fiefdom of advantaged blacks."[5] And the system worked, as Dunbar turned out the likes of not only Charles R. Drew, but of Dr. W. Montague Cobb, anatomist; Robert C. Weaver, secretary of housing and urban development in the cabinet of President Lyndon B. Johnson; Edward Brooke, former United States senator from Massachusetts; William Hastie, the first black to become a federal district court judge, who went on to become a federal appellate court judge; Charles H. Houston, vice-dean of the Howard University Law School; and Benjamin O. Davis, Sr., the first black general, among others. Ironically, the 1954 Supreme Court case of *Brown v. The Board of Education of Topeka Kansas* and the massive overhauling of the Washington, D.C., schools that followed it turned Dunbar into just another ghetto high school, scarcely distinguishable from hundreds of others.

At Dunbar Drew was a four-letter man, and he also found time in his senior year to serve as captain of Company B, Third Regiment, in the Cadet Corps. During his high school career he was at various times voted "best athlete," "most popular student," and "student who has done most for the school." Twice he was awarded the James E. Walker Medal for all-around athletic performance. It all led to an athletic scholarship to attend Amherst College, in Massachusetts, but that only covered part of his expenses.

Given his background—that is, the kind of neighborhood from which he came, the kind of family in which he was reared, and the kind of high school that he attended—Drew was never, from the day he was born, "a poor and disadvantaged little Negro boy, but one destined to succeed." Rather, he was just an American boy who was *expected* to succeed because there was no good reason why he should not. And he did.

Drew graduated from Dunbar High with the class of 1922. That year in Washington, the Lincoln Memorial, near Foggy Bottom, was dedicated. Negro ticket-holders who attended the ceremonies were required to sit in a roped-off section behind the whites, even though one of the featured speakers, along with President Warren

G. Harding and former President William Howard Taft, was Robert R. Moton, president of the Tuskegee Institute. Meanwhile, over at the Capitol, southern senators mounted a successful filibuster against the Dyer Anti-Lynching Bill. But for now and a while Drew was leaving all that. Ahead of him at Amherst were four more years of athletic distinction, years that also saw him set his feet on the path that led to his distinguished career in medicine.

NOTES

1. Interview with Mrs. Nora Gregory.

2. Ibid.

3. Ibid.

4. David L. Lewis, *District of Columbia: A Bicentennial History* (New York: Norton, 1976), 106–8. See also Thomas Sowell, *Black Education: Myths and Tragedies* (New York: McKay, 1972), 283–86.

5. Ibid., 108.

This chapter is based largely on an interview with Joseph L. Drew and his wife, Grace Ridgeley Drew, and another with Mrs. Nora Gregory. Mr. Drew and Mrs. Gregory are the brother and sister of Charles R. Drew. Also used were the following: Ben Richardson and William A. Fahey, *Great Black Americans,* 2d rev. ed. (New York: Crowell, 1976), 269; W. Montague Cobb, "Charles Richard Drew, M.D., 1904–1950," *Journal of the National Medical Association,* 42 (July, 1950): 239–42; Elmer DeGowin, Robert C. Hardin, and John B. Alsever, *Blood Transfusion* (Philadelphia: W.B. Saunders, Co., 1949), 1–2; Anne S. Bittker, "Charles Richard Drew, M.D.," *Negro History Bulletin,* 36 (Nov., 1973): 145; David Hepburn, "The Life of Dr. Charles R. Drew," *Our World* (July, 1950): 25.

CHAPTER

2

Coming of Age

The boy Charlie grew into a handsome man. He was tall—that much we know for sure. But just how tall he was is less certain. While an athlete at Amherst, he was described as being six feet, one inch tall, weighing 195 pounds, but a 1949 passport, supposedly bearing information that Drew himself furnished, gave his height as five feet, eleven inches. Twenty years after his death, his widow, Lenore, recalled him as being an even six feet tall, weighing 195 pounds, yet in his last photographs Drew seemed a portlier man than he was while an Amherst athlete. What can be said for certain, then, is that Charles R. Drew was a tall, solidly built man of approximately six feet, who weighed roughly two hundred pounds.

Given his mixed ancestry, it is not surprising that Drew had a complexion that was fair and somewhat freckled—"buttermilk-like," one friend recalled—but he could quickly redden when angered. His wife, Lenore, though, remembered his complexion as being "reddish, like an Irishman." And he had hair almost to match, which all agree was brown, though his widow says "reddish brown." It was also thin, and getting thinner, to his acknowledged discomfort, while his high brow exaggerated his balding appearance. At any rate, this big man, whether he only became red when angered or had naturally reddish skin and hair, was known later (not surprisingly) as "Big Red." His brown eyes were quite small, as can be seen in numerous photographs, while those who knew him and remember him also have described them as "sparkling," "twinkling," and "quick to light up." But the big man apparently did not have a big voice to go with his athlete's body. His brother, Joe, recalled that his voice was in the "medium range, tending to be higher when he was excited," while he might speak in a well-measured cadence, or much more rapidly, "depending on the subject matter."[1] An acquaintance of Drew's, who met him when he was a child in Canada, recalled the young American whom his father brought home for Sunday dinner, remarking a half century later, "I do remember being most impressed by Charles Drew's soft manner of speech."[2]

But perhaps none of this matters, least of all the contradictions. For what everyone saw was but the vessel. And what the photographs have preserved is but the image of that vessel. The man inside was much more complex and much more interesting.

In 1922, Drew was just a tall, well-built, good-looking Amherst College freshman, with a slightly quizzical but very serious (even somewhat pained) expression on his face. At least he appears so in all the photographs of him that survive from that era. Later, as Drew came to know his profession and who he was in that profession—indeed, as he probably came to know himself better—that somewhat troubled countenance softened and changed to one that obviously belonged to a happy, confident, and enthusiastic man. It is all there—in the photographs.

Amherst was, in many ways, the ideal educational world for Drew. One of the nation's better, if not best, liberal arts colleges, Amherst not only was as fine a place as any to get a first-rate education, in addition (and in keeping with the best classical or Greek tradition) it was a college that did not slight athletics, Drew's forte at the time. Also, even though Amherst was in New England, it was not as if he had gone so terribly far from home and loved ones, for among his classmates were at least two Washington friends— W. Montague Cobb, who became a distinguished anatomist and author and the editor of *The Journal of the National Medical Association,* and W. Mercer Cook, who became a French literary scholar and eventually served as United States ambassador to Niger and to Senegal. Together, Drew and Cook, while students at Amherst, wrote the fraternity hymn for Omega Psi Phi, the second oldest black college fraternity. And among the lifelong friends that Drew made at Amherst were two other black students—William H. Hastie, also a Dunbar alumnus (and, as noted in chapter 1, the first black appointed to a federal district court judgeship and then to a federal circuit court of appeals judgeship), and Ben Davis from Atlanta, later a New York City councilman. Amherst, Dartmouth, Williams, Oberlin, Harvard—all were favorites of the Washington, D.C., black elite.

Interestingly, only these close Amherst friends, and a few others, were ever addressed by Drew by their first names; all others he addressed by their surnames. Perhaps, but only perhaps, the more formal usage was a defense against possible rebuff because of Drew's race; certainly it would have hurt more to be snubbed by someone addressed on a first-name basis. On the other hand, the more formal usage simply may have fitted better with Drew's natural dignity—dignity that might not have wanted strangers to get too close.

Amherst thus furnished him an opportunity for making new friendships and for cultivating old ones; it was an opportunity for personal growth, and, of course, for a superior education, but it was also an opportunity to excel in what Drew at that time was best at—athletics, of nearly all kinds. In his first year he was the only freshman to win a major letter, which he earned in track; in his sophomore year he was a standout halfback on the football team; and in his junior year he was awarded the Thomas W. Ashley Memorial Trophy as the member of his class who had contributed the most to athletics. In 1925 he was chosen for honorable mention as an All-American halfback in the eastern division while he also successfully competed in the high hurdles and the high jump. Years after Drew's death, his old Amherst College football coach, D. O. ("Tuss") McLaughry, perhaps with a bit of hyperbole, said of him: "As a football player, Drew was great. He could have played regular on any team in the country, both in his era, and anytime since."[3]

Devoting so much time and energy to athletics led Drew to slight his studies, not that he was ever in serious academic trouble. But there is an apocryphal story on that point that well may be true. At any rate, a certain degree of neglect of his studies is said to have led to a conference in the dean's office and to a lecture in which Drew was told: "Mr. Drew, Negro athletes are a dime a dozen. Good day."[4] Drew nevertheless stuck to athletics, but he is supposed to have turned himself around as a student.

In 1926, graduation came for Drew, as it usually does to bright students, even when they apply themselves less than diligently. By then, influenced perhaps in part by the death of his sister Elsie in 1920 while he was still in high school, Drew had decided upon a career in medicine. But the money just was not there, which meant that he had to go to work to help pay for his medical studies; after all, he had received an athletic scholarship to Amherst, not an academic scholarship. With only an average academic record, but a superior one in athletics, it was natural that Coach McLaughry's stellar athlete should himself take to coaching,— which he did, at Morgan College in Baltimore, Maryland, with the title of Director of Athletics and Instructor in Biology and Chemistry, his best subjects at Amherst. The next two years Drew spent in Baltimore—teaching, trying to save a little money for medical school, and producing memorable teams in both football and basketball from what appeared to be only average raw material. Drew was that kind of coach; later he would become that kind of teacher and trainer of surgeons. He was able to inspire the merely competent to become good, the good to become better, and the better to become the best, whether on athletic fields, in medical school classrooms, or in hospital operating rooms.

Drew's first choice among possible medical schools was Howard University, at least partly because he could live at home then and save on expenses. But to his consternation, Howard denied him admission because he had taken only six credit hours in English at Amherst, not eight, as required. The blow was softened somewhat, however, and his ego salved when his rejection by Howard University's medical school was soon followed by an offer from the athletic department to hire him for the position of assistant football coach, with faculty rank! He declined the offer.

Drew was rankled, even angered by his rejection by the medical school. His brother, Joe, recalled in 1983 how Drew vowed, "Someday I'll come back here and run this damned place."[5] He did come back, and there were times when the dean of the medical school, and others, either feared that he would, or believed that he in fact did, run the place! When that day came, though, it was no longer that "damned place," for the Howard University Medical School and its affiliated teaching hospital, Freedmen's, eventually became home for him, and he became determined that they, together, could and would produce surgeons who were the equal of those trained anywhere else in the world.

But all that was years away, while the problem now was where he might go to medical school. With his sights set high, as always, Drew applied to McGill University, in Montreal, Canada. The Canadians were not so picky about their English requirements, and they were obviously satisfied with the rest of his academic record at Amherst, too, for he was accepted. So, in the autumn of 1928, Drew headed north for what was to become the most color-blind experience of his life.

At this stage of his education, one might have thought that Drew's athletic career, if not his athletic interests, would be behind him, but not so, for in Canadian universities of that day, students in the graduate and professional schools were eligible to compete in intercollegiate athletics if they wished to do so. Drew did, and he won Canadian championships in both the high and low hurdles and in the high jump and broad jump as well! In 1944, more than ten years after he had graduated from McGill, and after he had achieved some measure of fame as a medical scientist and surgeon, Drew returned to McGill University for a football game. At the halftime it was announced over the public address system that "Charlie Drew is in the stands," at which, according to his widow, Lenore, "the audience exploded with applause and everyone was on his feet."[6] That Canadian crowd certainly was not cheering a black American surgeon—they were cheering Charlie Drew, the famed McGill University athlete. No wonder Drew would come to say, many times, with the desire to get others to rank his achievements as he had, that one of the two things he could never live down was football. The other, blood plasma research, as he approached medical school as a first-year student, was still ahead of him.

It was money, though, more than the disciplinary or the intellectual challenge of medical school, that was the main problem facing Drew. So, in the classical tradition of the struggling university student of that day, he took a job waiting tables for his fellow students. But even that was not enough, so when his old coach, "Tuss"

McLaughry, learned of Drew's predicament in a letter from him, he raised several hundred dollars as a loan from among Drew's former classmates at Amherst. At the time Drew still had outstanding a $250 loan, with an interest charge, from Amherst College, since neither his scholarship nor his father's help had been enough to meet all his expenses. But the late-blooming intellectual was finally coming into flower, so that in Drew's third year at McGill his financial worries were eased somewhat by the award of a scholarship. In his senior (or fifth) year, based upon the results of a competitive examination among the top five members of the graduating class, Drew was awarded the Williams Prize for excellence. Earlier he had been elected to membership in Alpha Omega Alpha, the honorary scholastic fraternity for medical students.

But merely recounting Drew's academic story this way makes it all sound so simple—the triumph of another poor medical student as a result of his own perseverance and hard work, with a helping hand from some old friends. The price paid was much greater than that, and probably no one but Charlie Drew ever knew that price, unless his widow or children happened to read, among the papers he left behind at his death, a long handwritten soliloquy by him. Amounting to some eight typewritten double-spaced pages when transcribed, it was addressed to nobody by name; instead, it was apparently addressed to the New Year, 1930 (but that does not become obvious until the last paragraph on the last page). Dated "12:30 A.M., January 1, 1930," the composition runs like this:

> What a hell of a New Year! As the year entered [I] was paying the cashier at the Northeastern Lunch. Ten cents for tea and toast. I was cold from walking all over the city—looking for what? I don't know. Excitement maybe, trouble—most anything out of the ordinary just like the hordes I passed—some laughing young couples—they looked the happiest, other more elderly couples—out seeking a return of the youth from which they had drawn away with the passage of days—days which had turned their temples grey and slowed their steps.

Here was a lonely man, but here, too, was a man with great powers of observation and language, attempting to record, if painfully, the human condition of a perhaps not so atypical New Year's Eve. He continued somewhat more optimistically, but not for long: "Today

I haven't been hungry. I was well dressed. I am not sick and have no great sorrow, yet I have felt poverty today as I have never felt it before. I have a dollar. Tonight I wanted to join the merry-making in some form or another so bad that my very heart ached. I couldn't go very far on a dollar, not even alone, and solitude is the only thing I enjoy alone."

But that night he didn't want solitude. He wanted "companions, gay companions, girls and fellows"—also, perhaps, "a stolen kiss in the middle of a dance." In this vein he sensuously wandered on with such expressions as "hair that is soft to the touch and sweet smelling" (brown, black, or blonde hair, the color did not matter, he wrote), "brown eyes that have that merry twinkle . . . black eyes that intrigue," or blue eyes "like the angels must have," or indeed, "any kind of eyes," he despairingly wrote. There was more; then he turned again to hunger: "I have a dollar—I am afraid to spend it—tomorrow I must eat and the day after, and many days after that. . . . For days now I have not been sure whether I would eat or not. Tomorrow I know I will because I have been invited to dinner, but the next day?"

That night Drew laid his soul bare as few men or women ever do, whether in writing or in conversation with another. So far, in less than half the soliloquy, he had written of despair and loneliness; of poverty, passion, and desire; and of hunger, always hunger—the fear of physical hunger and the reality of hunger for human companionship. Then, at the halfway mark, pride raised its head:

> I never ask favors. That is one of the things I am proud of. Rightly or wrongly proud, I don't know. This I know—that this pride sustains me when otherwise I would sink. . . . My classmates today could not understand why I wouldn't go to the dance with them tonight. When I told them frankly that I was broke, they simply thought I had over-spent my allowance or my check hadn't come in, or something to that effect. They didn't understand that while $10 to some of them will mean—well, just $10 and maybe a note to Dad, that to me it means a whole week's living, or from my father it would mean an actual sacrifice for the rest of my family.

One of Drew's classmates even offered to pay his way and could not understand why his offer was refused. But to Drew, it was a matter of simple pride, and the desire for independence.

If I accept gifts without the potentiality of repaying them I give up a part of my independence, I become indebted. My independence I must maintain [for] as long as I am not obligated to anyone in any way even poverty does not make me humble [for] as a man, I am the equal of any man I meet. . . . When I allow myself to become obligated, I put myself in a position in which my judgments may become prejudiced by those obligations.

Of course, Drew already was indebted at the time to his family, to Coach McLaughry and some of his old Amherst classmates who had loaned him money, and to Amherst College for a student loan. At about this point in his soliloquy he noted that he had been writing for three hours, but he had much more to say. He went on, touching on poverty again, and more poverty, of how he once pawned—but recovered—his tuxedo and his suitcase. Finally, if he were hungry enough, he admitted, "I have no doubt but that I would steal."

Then, no longer defiant, but despairing, he wrote, "Yet here I am: a stranger amongst strangers in a strange land, broke, busted, almost disgusted, doing my family no good, myself little that is now demonstrable. Yet I know I must go on somehow—I must finish what I have started." And finally, he spoke to the New Year directly:

I am sleepy now, so Babe, 1930 looks like the going is going to be hard for you as far as I am concerned. Your birth was under an ominous sky, your early moments most inauspicious, you do not look a bit healthy, but I am going to try like the devil to make something out of you. Maybe your prognosis isn't as fatalistic as the present diagnosis indicates, but do not expect anything sudden or big to happen. Got to handle you awful carefully. I won't have to make many slips to make you count for naught, so if you have any good luck with you spread it on thick or I might lose you. I will check up with you in twelve months. In closing, I must say again—this is one hell of a New Year's Day![7]

Despite Drew's promise, there is no record of a similar lengthy address to "New Year 1931." By then, with the receipt of a Rosenwald scholarship of $1,000 in the fall of 1930, life was undoubtedly more promising for Drew, and poverty less real. But at 12:30 A.M., New Year's Day, 1930, Drew could not see that far ahead. That New Year's Day he went out to the dinner to which he had been invited, and in a few days he was back at his medical studies, and perhaps at athletics as well.

At McGill, as at Amherst, Drew made several lifelong friendships. Even so, others whom he did not know well, or who were ahead of him or behind him in the course of their medical studies, nevertheless clearly remembered him a half century later. Among his friends was Dr. Richard B. Dunn, now retired, a white Greensboro, North Carolina, gynecologist. Drew and Dunn were in the same class, and because both their last names started with the letter *D*, alphabetical arrangement in classrooms and laboratories threw them together regularly. But they were also friends socially, and Dr. Dunn recalled how he and Charlie, alone or sometimes with others, regularly visited a favorite student haunt known as Kaufman's, whose specialty was "pigs' knuckles and beer." From his hospital bed in Greensboro, where he was recovering from back surgery, Dr. Dunn recalled, fifty years after he had last seen Charlie, the charming, cheerful, and delightful young man who, by sheer force of personality, stood out in whatever group he happened to be in at the moment. Dr. Dunn also remembered that Charlie was always near, or at, the top of his class.

Drew likewise met a lifelong friend in one of his instructors, Dr. John Beattie, an Englishman temporarily teaching at McGill, not much older than Drew himself. Beattie taught Drew bacteriology and reputedly was responsible for whetting his pupil's interest in blood research. Later, back in England, Beattie became director of the research laboratories of the Royal College of Surgeons, and early in World War II he was appointed director of the British Blood Transfusion Service.

In 1933, Drew was awarded the M.D.C.M. degree (Doctor of Medicine and Master of Chirurgie, or Surgery) by McGill University. The following academic year, 1933–34, he did his internship at the Royal Victoria Hospital and also did a general rotating internship at Montreal General Hospital. The next year, 1934–35, he stayed on at the Montreal General Hospital as a resident in medicine.

Upon completion of his residency in 1935, two things—the death of his father and the desire "to help his people"—led Drew to apply for an appointment to the medical faculty of Howard University in his hometown of Washington, D.C. This time, unlike the time he applied for admission as a medical student, Howard did not turn him down, and he was appointed to an instructorship in pathology at a salary of $150 a month, which was not a whole lot more than he had made as a teenager hustling newspapers.

So now it was south, home to Washington, D.C. and Howard University, the institution that would claim Drew's loyalty for the rest of his life despite ample, lucrative opportunities to move on.

NOTES

1. Joseph L. Drew to the author, June 30, 1983.

2. Frank R. N. Gurd to Lenore Drew, March 3, 1978, CRD Papers.

3. D. O. ("Tuss") McLaughry to Richard Hardwick, August 17, 1976, CRD Papers.

4. Hamilton Bims, "Charles Drew's 'Other' Medical Revolution," *Ebony*, 30 (Feb., 1974): 88.

5. Interview with Joseph L. Drew.

6. Lenore Drew, "Listen, My Children" (handwritten reminiscence, dated 1970), CRD Papers.

7. Charles R. Drew, "New Year's Day, 1930, Musings," CRD Papers.

The general notes for this chapter include the following: Charles R. Drew passport, June 9, 1949, CRD Papers; Lenore Drew, "Listen, My Children"; "Dr. Charles R. Drew," *The McGill News,* 31 (Summer, 1950): 56; David Hepburn, "The Life of Dr. Charles R. Drew," *Our World* (July, 1950): 25; reminiscences of E. King Graves, May 6, 1947, Amherst College Archives; W. Montague Cobb, "Charles Richard Drew, M.D., 1904–1950," *Journal of the National Medical Association*, 42 (July, 1950): 240–42; D. O. ("Tuss") McLaughry, "The Best Player I Ever Coached," *Saturday Evening Post,* 225 (Dec. 6, 1952): 184; interview with Dr. Richard E. Dunn.

3

Howard University and
Freedmen's Hospital

Howard University to which Drew came in 1935 was—and remains—a unique educational institution. It is private, but it always
has received the major portion of its operating funds from the federal government. And though from its inception Howard was open
to all races and creeds, enrollment has always been largely black,
though it is less so today than at any other time in its history.
Freedmen's Hospital, the teaching and clinical facility for the Howard University Medical School, on the other hand, was strictly federal until 1967, when its control and operation were transferred
to Howard University.

Unlike so many of the nation's universities, Howard was envisioned as a university from the beginning; it was never just a college that grew into a university, even if all its separate schools or
colleges did not begin at the same time. The charter founding
Howard University was enacted by Congress on March 2, 1867,
and was signed into law by President Andrew Johnson on the same
day. It stipulated that the university "shall consist of the following departments, and such others, as the Board of Trustees may
establish—first, normal; second, collegiate; third, theological;
fourth, law; fifth, medicine; sixth, agriculture."[1] By 1869 all those
departments, and a commercial department, were established,
though agriculture existed in name only and never developed a
curriculum.

Howard University was named for General Oliver Otis Howard,

the commissioner of the Freedmen's Bureau and longtime abolitionist. A native of Maine and the son of missionary parents, Howard was a graduate of the United States Military Academy and served in the Civil War from the very first battle, Bull Run; at the war's end he was commander of the Army of the Tennessee. He was a member of the original board of trustees of the university named for him, and in 1869 he became its third president, after Byron Sutherland (the first, Charles B. Boynton, lasted only 150 days). General Howard held the post till December 25, 1874.

Not till 1926 did Howard get its first black president, Mordecai Johnson. He served till 1960—thirty-four years in all. A native of Paris, Tennessee, Johnson was a graduate of Atlanta Baptist College (which in 1913 became Morehouse College). He subsequently received a second A.B. degree from the University of Chicago, a B.D. from Rochester Theological Seminary, and an S.T.M. from Harvard. It was during the controversial and stormy Johnson years that Howard achieved true national and international stature.

Johnson had been president for almost ten years when Charles R. Drew joined the medical faculty, and he was president for ten more years after Drew's death. Sometimes admired, often hated, almost always exasperating, Johnson could, in one of his "messianic moments," according to the late Howard University historian Rayford W. Logan—who himself had his differences with the president—tell the distinguished sociologist E. Franklin Frazier the kind of sociology he should write, and the economist Abram Harris the kind of economics he should study! To many, including perhaps Johnson himself, Johnson *was* Howard University.

It should be pointed out, however, to give justice to Johnson and also put him in proper perspective, that virtually all black colleges and universities in the United States have, at one time or another, experienced such an authoritarian stage of leadership, while the best-known black college president of them all, Booker T. Washington, was also the most authoritarian. But, where Johnson truly brought Howard University into the middle of the twentieth century, Washington, in the opinion of his critics, was content to leave (or at least resigned to leaving) Tuskegee in the nineteenth. Yet both were, perhaps, just what their respective institutions needed at the time.

Whatever their color, the chief problem facing all Howard presidents was finances. For instance, so precarious was federal support that until 1928 nearly every year the House of Representatives, as a "point of order," would strike Howard University's funds from the budget, and then, by tacit agreement, the Senate would put them back! As late as 1900 Howard received from Congress only $35,000 for current operating expenses. So erratic and uneven was that support that in 1908 the amount was $63,200, while it "soared" to $162,200 in 1909, and then fell back to $104,735 in 1910, and $92,000 in 1911! No university president could plan anything in the face of such erratic year-to-year support. Not till 1930 did the amount appropriated pass one million dollars— $1,249,000 in 1930, $1,760,000 in 1931—but only $675,000 in 1932, and then back up to $1,092,500 in 1933. But in 1934, notwithstanding New Deal deficit budgets, it fell to $665,241, with only minor increases for several years thereafter, so that the million-dollar mark was not passed again till 1943. And in 1950, the year Drew died, Congress budgeted a total of only $4,262,000 for the university's current operating expenses.

The story of congressional appropriations for capital expenditures is somewhat different, but only for the early years, when Howard was under the Freedmen's Bureau. By 1872, the year the bureau closed down, Congress had, up to that point, contributed $520,956 to the fledgling university. Then hard times followed: for instance, $3,500 was appropriated for the water system in 1883, and $400 for fire escapes in 1888. That was the story until 1909, when $95,000 was allotted for the science building to be built and furnished; in 1920, $85,000 was budgeted for the home economics building; in 1928, $370,000 for a medical building; and finally, in 1936, $1,120,812 for the impressive Founders' Library in the heart of the campus. Even so, by the time Drew died, Congress had never appropriated more than $2.6 million for capital expenditures in any one year.

Of course, there were other sources for funds, but none were large, and none were reliable on a continuing basis. For example, there were gifts from home and from abroad, and in the early years there were funds received from the sale of surplus land. Also, of course, there were tuition charges, but they were nominal.

Flush times did not really come to Howard University until the 1960s, a generally prosperous decade for nearly all colleges and universities.

The medical school, as a part of the general university, was also a victim of the university's financial straits. But the medical school had ties to another institution that was perhaps even more nearly starved to death—its teaching and clinical facility, Freedmen's Hospital, which operated under the auspices of the United States Department of the Interior.

Freedmen's (spelled with an *a* until 1869) Hospital was five years older than Howard University. The outbreak of the Civil War saw a great increase in the number of Negroes in Washington, with most of the increase consisting of destitute, runaway slaves, especially from Virginia, just across the Potomac River. Naturally, health problems arose, so in 1862 the federal government organized a medical aid camp, located at R and S Streets and Twelfth and Thirteenth Streets, NW. It was built over a former brickyard and a cemetery and was either mired in mud or smothered in dust. The next year the camp was named Freedman's, and a black surgeon, Major Alexander T. Augusta (later Lieutenant Colonel), was placed in charge. Although he was an officer, and one of eight black doctors commissioned during the war, Augusta received the pay of a common soldier.

In 1865 the buildings on the original site, such as they were, were razed, and the "hospital" moved to Vermont Avenue, between L and N Streets, NW. Later that same year it merged with the Campbell Hospital, located at the corner of Seventh Street and what is now Florida Avenue, NW. Finally, in 1869, Freedmen's was moved onto the campus of Howard University into buildings erected for it by the Freedmen's Bureau. The main building, made of brick and four stories high, was located at W and Fourth Streets, NW, with four frame buildings to serve as wards situated next to it. That year it also became the teaching hospital for the new Howard University Medical School. And for long it was the only District of Columbia hospital where black physicians could treat private patients.

The new facilities were not, of course, "built for the ages," and Washington, including its black population, was growing. In a few years there was a crying need for new and enlarged quarters, but it was a need long ignored. An official investigation of conditions in 1898 found the wood-built wards to be firetraps, the plumbing inadequate and unsanitary, and the hospital's entire supply of surgical instruments not much more than an ordinary stock for the average country physician. Even so, five more years elapsed before Congress, in March 1903, appropriated $350,000 for the construction of a new hospital, to be located just north of Pomeroy Street, a stone's throw from the old hospital. It was still another five years before the new and modern facility (which ultimately cost $500,000) opened in February 1908. Four years later, in June 1912, Freedmen's ceased functioning as a strictly charity hospital when treatment of paying patients was authorized.

But modern hospitals require major expenditures to keep them modern; since such expenditures were made impossible by a parsimonious Congress, in a few years the "new Freedmen's" was well on its way to becoming the "Jim Crow shack" that President Mordecai Johnson repeatedly called it. Others used stronger terms, such as "a dump," "a national disgrace," and so on. Not surprisingly, there was undoubtedly some credence to the stories told by black taxi drivers and others who took sick and injured patients there in spite of their cries, "Don't take me to Freedmen's. I'll die."[2] Others, though, felt about Freedmen's as the widow of the man who was to become the hospital's most famous surgeon did. Mrs. Charles R. Drew recalled how, even in its worst days, the black community looked upon Freedmen's as its own. It was the one hospital in Washington where, when a black female patient entered, "You were called Miss Jones [e.g.] and treated with respect."[3]

This, then, was the kind of teaching and clinical facility that for too long was the only one available to the medical school of Howard University, which, in turn, was also inadequately supported, as already described. But unlike the hospital, the university at least could look to private resources as well as public ones. Also, healthy university students, there by choice, obviously did not suffer from the inadequate support and facilities in the same way as the sick and injured did, who were brought to the "Jim Crow shack" by circumstance.

In the end, just as President Mordecai Johnson was able (albeit with a heavy hand) to bring Howard University into the mainstream of higher education, so was Dean Numa P. G. Adams able to do the same with the medical school, even if he did not have the iron hide and constitution of President Johnson. In fact, the job and the struggle probably hastened his death. As with the presidency of the university, until the appointment of Dean Adams, a white man had always been dean. Now, with Johnson, the first black president, it was not surprising that black appointees began to be moved into key administrative positions, such as the deanship of the medical school. In fact, this was part of a national trend among black colleges. White paternalism was being rejected, and blacks were insisting upon moving to the fore in leading their own institutions.

Unfortunately for Dean Adams, he was not the first choice for his post, and knowledge of that fact undoubtedly made his task more difficult. It was true that President Johnson had not been the first choice for his post, either, but what Johnson lacked in a mandate, he made up for in sheer force of personality and in a way with words that put his less verbally gifted opponents at great disadvantage. Dean Adams, on the other hand, was a quiet man with sober, steady ways, ill-suited by temperament for the sort of academic infighting upon which President Johnson seemed to thrive. But Adams knew what he wanted, and he knew what was needed to give stature to the medical school—and he succeeded. Indeed, had it not been apparent by 1935, when Drew joined the medical faculty, that a new day was dawning for Howard University, he probably never would have applied. Dean Adams thus played no small part in what the Howard University Medical School accomplished and what it became, and he was also instrumental in attracting the likes of Drew and then seeing that their training was furthered (aware of the advantages that this would have for his school's reputation).

Numa P. G. Adams was born on February 26, 1885, in the Virginia hamlet of Delaplane, located in Fauquier County about fifty miles west of Washington, D.C. Though it was a tiny place, all his life Adams returned there for comfort and solace whenever he felt the need. At age thirteen, his parents moved to Steelton, Pennsylvania, where he graduated from high school in 1905. After two years as a substitute teacher in Steelton and Carlisle, Pennsylvania, he enrolled at Howard University, from which he graduated magna cum laude in 1911. He next earned a master's degree in chemistry from Columbia University and then returned to Howard, where from 1912 to 1919 he served successively as instructor, assistant professor, and then associate professor, while in his last year he served as department head as well. In September 1919, he left Howard to attend Rush Medical College in Chicago, from which he graduated in 1923, and began an internship at St. Louis Hospital, No. 2 (later the Homer G. Phillips Hospital). An honor graduate, he was (like Drew) a member of Alpha Omega Alpha, the honorary medical scholastic fraternity. Adams started a practice in Chicago, but shortly after joined the Victory Life Insurance Company as assistant medical director. From 1927 to 1929 he also served as an instructor of neurology and psychiatry at the Provident Hospital School of Nursing.

When four other prominent black physicians—Dr. Louis T. Wright of New York, Dr. William A. Hinton of Boston, Dr. Charles H. Garvin of Cleveland, and Dr. Julian H. Lewis of Chicago—all turned down the offer of appointment as dean of the medical school at Howard, the handsome, shy, and retiring Adams was left to fill the post. Thus it was that the music-loving Adams (he had played both the cornet and the saxophone professionally in Washington and Chicago) took on the task of becoming the first black dean.

When Dean Adams arrived on campus he had the advantage of recently improved facilities, for in 1927 a new half-million-dollar medical building was opened, made possible by a $250,000 fund-raising campaign that was matched by the General Education Board of the Rockefeller Foundation. However, buildings alone could not make a respected medical school, so Dean Adams set out to raise the quality of both the students and faculty. To enhance the quality of the student body he sought to reduce the size of the beginning medical classes rather than change the rules or the standards for those students already there. Because of the great need for more, not fewer, Negro physicians, it was a move that was widely opposed, both from within and from without the university. But Adams won this quality versus quantity tug-of-war.

The task of improving the faculty, though, was more difficult, if less emotional, and it could not be solved in short order, what with both tradition and powerful, entrenched interests to fight. For instance, before 1912 the medical school operated on a nighttime schedule, a practice that assuredly did not exist for the benefit of students who had jobs during the day. Rather, teaching at Howard amounted to moonlighting for the faculty, whether white or black (and there were both). Their private practices came first. By the time Dean Adams arrived, classes still were scheduled frequently for the very early hours (*before* private practice) or late in the afternoon (*after* private practice). Also, the white faculty, whether numerically superior or not, usually determined larger policy and held most of the department headships. Under the new dean, classes began to be scheduled for the convenience of the students, while here and there more black department heads began to appear.

Dean Adams then proceeded to persuade the Rockefeller General Education Board, already the medical school's chief benefactor, to put up the money for two-year, as opposed to one-year, fellowships for the training of outstanding faculty members. (See the next chapter for details of the Howard University–Rockefeller Foundation relationship.) At the same time, Adams urged—even leaned on—the fortunate recipients of the two-year fellowships to register for and pursue the Ph.D. degree in their fields. Drew was one of the first two fellows selected for this additional training. In addition to the fellowships, Adams also persuaded the General Education Board of the Rockefeller Foundation to fund two outstanding white professors, one in surgery and one in medicine, to be on the medical school faculty for five years. He wanted them to modernize the organization and operation of the various departments, to work with and train black physicians already on the faculty, and then to recommend the best ones for the fellowships.

Together, President Johnson and Dean Adams brought heady times to Howard University, especially to the medical school, but where Johnson seemed to thrive on the difficulties of the task, with Adams it seemed they took their toll. For instance, Adams not only had to fight an entrenched medical establishment and all the "old ways" of doing things, he also had to serve two masters, as it were, with one master, the university, a private institution, and the other, Freedmen's, federal. At the same time, he had to struggle to get them to work for the common goal of both better care for Freedmen's Hospital patients and better training for Howard University medical students and residents. But succeed he did, and to the Howard medical faculty came men like Drew, James R. Laurey, and

John B. Manley, to name only three. They were also the first black physicians to be selected for the two-year residency training. In turn, they would come back to Howard to do the kind of teaching and training for which Drew especially became famous.

Adams lived to see Drew and Laurey return to Howard, but on August 29, 1941, he died, with his work unfinished, still longing for his beloved Delaplane, where he had intended to retire and build a home. It was to his and to President Johnson's Howard University that Drew had come home, whether or not he realized it.

NOTES

1. Rayford W. Logan, *Howard University: The First Hundred Years, 1867–1967* (New York: New York University Press, 1969), 22.

2. Hamilton Bims, "Charles Drew's 'Other' Medical Revolution," *Ebony*, 30 (Feb., 1974): 91.

3. *Washington Post*, March 2, 1975.

W. Montague Cobb, "Numa P. G. Adams, M.D., 1885–1940," *Journal of the National Medical Association*, 43 (Jan., 1951): 46–52; *Washington Post*, March 2, 1975; Logan, *Howard University*, 40–41; Thomas Holt, Casandra Smith-Parker, and Rosalyn Terborg-Penn, *A Special Mission: The Story of Freedmen's Hospital, 1862–1962* (Washington: Academic Affairs Division, Howard University, 1975).

The Rockefeller Foundation and Howard University

The quality of medical education and training in the United States at the dawn of the twentieth century ranged all the way from "world class" at such institutions as Harvard and Johns Hopkins to that of "deplorably disgraceful" at perhaps dozens of others. Any approximation of fairly uniform standards was missing, from admission to medical school to graduation from medical school. The result was that incompetency was probably more of a threat to the public than quackery. In 1910, Abraham Flexner, sponsored by the Carnegie Foundation for the Advancement of Teaching, researched and wrote *Medical Education in the United States and Canada.* Flexner reported that conditions in some so-called medical schools were "shocking." Dirty, unsanitary "death traps," he called many of them. Even high school dropouts, he found, were "earning" medical degrees at some of the more notorious proprietary institutions. Flexner had visited every one of the 155 medical schools in the United States and Canada and he described each in detail. He recommended that 120 of them be closed. Most soon were, or else they died from the publicity. Five were schools for blacks.

No profession could maintain either its dignity or its integrity in the face of such criticism without seeking change and improvement. Belatedly, then, the American Medical Association set about cleaning up its own house by establishing accreditation standards. Soon medical schools either were classified "A," for accredited, or "B," which was a provisional status with fixed time limits. There were to be no permanent classifications of "B" and "C" grade, though of course there were gradations of quality among the "A"-rated schools, just as there are today. But all schools had to—as all now must—meet a certain acceptable standard for accreditation.

Not surprisingly, black medical training was hurt the worst of all. White medical students at least had some good publicly owned, as well as privately owned, institutions open to them; many of these were in fact closed to blacks, or else severely limited in black enrollment. For instance, for the academic year 1919–20, there were only thirty-nine black students enrolled, at all levels, in predominantly nonblack medical schools in the whole United States, none of them in the South. Rush Medical School, in Chicago, had the largest number, seven; Northwestern, also in Chicago, had five; Boston University, four; and Harvard and the University of Pennsylvania, three each. The only publicly supported medical education for blacks, in a black setting, was at Howard University, and in the preceding chapter we saw what a starvation level of support that was at. The only privately supported, predominantly black medical schools still operating at that time (1919–20) were Meharry Medical College, in Nashville, Tennessee, and Leonard Medical School of Shaw University, in Raleigh, North Carolina. And Leonard was soon to fold. In a sense, black medical education was worse off in 1920 than it had been in 1900, when, in addition to Howard and Meharry and the white medical schools that accepted an occasional Negro student, there had been five weak black institutions (since closed) that had turned out at least the semblance of physicians. Now, in 1920, there was even increased competition among whites for the fewer openings that generally existed in medical schools in the wake of dozens of closed schools.

Then, too, racism in the nation was at or near its height: five years earlier, in 1915, the Ku Klux Klan had experienced a revival, only this time it was a national, not just a southern, phenomenon. Also, that same year witnessed the following turn of events: Thomas Dixon's highly racist novel about reconstruction after the Civil War, *The Clansman*, leapt into public prominence through one of the most famous films of all time, *The Birth of a Nation;* racial segregation in the South had, over the past thirty years, matured into two separate worlds, one black and one white; and the problem of residential segregation in the northern cities was being aggravated by the influx of thousands of blacks who were leaving the South for the North. Meanwhile, with the inauguration of Woodrow Wilson as president in 1913, the nation had at its helm the first southerner, by birth and rearing, since Andrew Johnson, who took office just after the Civil War. Under Wilson and his largely southern cabinet, racial segregation even came to the federal offices in the nation's capital. For the Negro American, this era was truly the nadir: he could either stay at the bottom, or he could go up, but with no abolitionists and reconstructionists, such as the nineteenth century had, to show the way through public policy, where could he turn, except to the interracial, fledgling National Association for the Advancement of Colored People? Anyway, it was now public policy, both state and federal, to keep the Negro *down*.

This was where the new age of private philanthropy came in— funded by the huge fortunes made possible by the hands-off policy of the federal government toward private wealth and the absence of income taxes for more than a generation after the Civil War. Men of goodwill now came to the fore with money—money to tackle the problems of health, education, and training at all levels for black and white alike. And for now, at least, in the wake of Booker T. Washington's accomodationist and separatist philosophy, it did not seem to matter that this aid was rendered in a segregationist framework. Carnegie, Peabody, Jeanes, and Rosenwald, among others, were names that soon meant, in the new century, opportunity and advancement for the disadvantaged, whether of a region or of a race. But no name, no philanthropy, stood out more than that of Rockefeller, with the Rockefeller Foundation and the General Education Board (GEB) that the foundation later funded. From its inception in 1903, the GEB was supported by funds supplied directly by John D. Rockefeller, Sr. After 1913, the year the Rockefeller Foundation was created, GEB support came from the foundation. Here was black medical education's way out of the wilderness.

Endowments, and the income generated by them, are the financial key to the development that lies behind the greatness of any insti-

tution. Thus it was that on April 19, 1912, the medical school of
Howard University first approached the General Education Board,
headquartered in New York City, for help in raising an endowment
of a million dollars, soon scaled down to a half million. It was a
long, slow, and tedious process, and both sides had a lot to learn
about each other. Officials at Howard overshot the mark, in the
opinion of GEB officials, when they sought to make comparisons
between Harvard University's medical school, that of Johns Hopkins University, and Howard's, whether they referred to the present state of Howard's medical school or to what it might become.
Big dreams, if not the means to see them through, came easily. This
led to polite but firm chiding in some of the correspondence directed to Howard by GEB officials. With good grace the criticism
was accepted, and consequent directions complied with. After all,
officials at Howard soon learned what both earlier and later sup-
plicants to philanthropic foundations have had to learn: "He who
pays the piper. . . ." Paternalism, too, raised its head from time to
time in correspondence directed to Howard by the GEB, but then
one must remember that the civil rights revolution was a generation away, and paternalism then was often accepted by both sides
as a way of life that governed racial relationships.

Not until February 26, 1920, almost eight years after Howard's
initial request, did the GEB approve a grant of $250,000—half the
prospective endowment of $500,000—contingent upon Howard
University Medical School's raising the other half from other
sources. Howard had until July 1, 1926—six years—to raise its
half, but that deadline later had to be extended to December
31, 1927. The GEB stipulated that the income from the endowment was to be used for the improvement of teaching in the fundamental branches of medicine, and for equipment and full-time
assistants.

This was the beginning of a long and supportive relationship
between Howard and the GEB. Before that relationship termi-
nated, in 1942, practically every facet of the medical school's ac-
tivities—construction, equipment, additional training for faculty,
administrative support, clinical teaching, the library, and so on—
was touched by the GEB and Rockefeller funds, to the tune of
$634,000, a sum that may not seem so large anymore, but one
that, in terms of today's dollars, would be in the millions. It was a

major contribution by any standard, and it was the one above all others that prepared the Howard University Medical School to take advantage of the funding sources (largely public) of the 1960s and 1970s. It should be pointed out that at this time, Meharry, the other black medical school (located in Nashville, Tennessee) was also receiving GEB support, but on a much more massive scale, to the tune of $8,670,000 over the years, some fourteen times as much money as the GEB awarded Howard. But then, unlike Howard, Meharry did not have the federal government to look to for the major portion of its support. Besides, Meharry was located in the South, not in the nation's capital. Both the need for help and the opportunity to do good well may have appeared greater there.

Even before the initial GEB grant of $250,000 was fully matched, the board cast another vote of confidence in Howard University when, in 1927, it awarded $130,000 toward construction of a new half-million-dollar medical building. The federal government provided $370,000 of the total amount, and the GEB grant rounded out the needed funds. As evidence that the GEB viewed assistance to the Howard University Medical School as an ongoing commitment—one from the ground up, through the wards, and into the operating rooms—Henry S. Pritchett of the GEB, on March 19, 1929, wrote: "The GEB is committed to a program of building, maintenance, and eventual endowment" of the Howard University Medical School. As part of that ongoing commitment, that same year the GEB granted the medical school another $75,000, for a five-year program of advanced training for four of its faculty—in anatomy, preventive medicine and public health, pharmacology, and pathology. At about the same time, the GEB committed itself to funding, for four years, Dean Numa P. Adams's salary of $6,500 a year, and $1,000 a year for travel. Then in 1930, a grant of $5,000 was made for a survey of the medical library's resources and for new acquisitions. Funds for the endowment, for advanced training, for administrative expenses, for buildings, and for the library—all were there by 1930, in a comprehensive and well-thought-out aid package, at the insistence of the GEB.

Dean Adams's full-time staff was aging, and as late as 1935 there still were employed a few physicians whose tenure dated back to the last years of the nineteenth century. Adams decided that new blood of the very first quality was needed, especially in the two major departments of medicine and surgery. New department heads who would bring new life to those departments by both precept and example were his next priority. So when the five-year training program that the GEB funded in 1929 ended in 1934, Dean Adams once more approached the board.

Already he had, for more than a year, been searching for really first-class black department heads for the departments of medicine and surgery, but without success. So, on January 25, 1935, in an interview with Dr. Robert A. Lambert of the GEB, Adams declared that he had come around to the view that he preferred white men for the job anyway—and this from the first black dean that the Howard University Medical School had ever had. Adams told Lambert that reluctantly he had concluded that the appointment of two white men would cause less "trouble" than would the appointment of black department heads, due to "local, professional jealousies." Adams was seeking a total of $100,000 for a five-year program, or $50,000 for each of the two department heads. At $10,000 a year, this broke down into an annual salary of $7,500, $500 for a resident in training, and $2,000 for equipment, travel, and other miscellaneous expenses. Adams was successful in his quest, and beginning on July 1, 1936, the funds became available from the GEB.

Early in the search for the new head of surgery, the name of Dr. Edward Lee Howes, research assistant in surgery at Yale, surfaced, and there were never any other serious contenders. Honest, forthright, candid to the point of bluntness, a man of high standards and great organizing ability, Howes frequently was regarded as a diamond in the rough, or simply, the rough-and-ready type. A graduate of Yale, with both B.S. and M.D. degrees from that institution and a Doctor of Science degree from Columbia University followed by additional study in Germany and France, Howes was only thirty-three years old when he came to Howard. In fact, he was just a year older than the man who would become his first resident, and later his successor, at Howard—Charles Richard Drew.

Along with Howes, but after a more difficult search, Dr. Raymond L. Gregory, assistant professor of medicine at Louisiana State University, was appointed to head the Department of Medicine. A native of Texas and a graduate of the University of Texas with an M.D. degree from the University of Minnesota, Gregory, aged thirty-six, never quite caught on at Howard like the rough-and-ready Howes, and three years later, in 1939, while the GEB grant still had two years to run, he was lured away from Howard by a better offer.

Howes, too, at the end of his first year at Howard, was tempted to leave because of the inadequate equipment and nursing service, dirty wards, and frequent lack of towels, saline and glucose solutions, tetanus anti-toxin, and so on. But he stayed, and, perhaps because of his tough and blunt ways, he came to be admired and even loved. After all, though they often complained about it, the medical faculty at Howard had become accustomed to dealing with such superiors in the persons of Dean Adams and President Mordecai Johnson, both of whom ran their bailiwicks as if they were fiefdoms.

When Howes was approved by the GEB and the Howard University Board of Trustees and given a five-year contract with the medical school, it was with the understanding that at the end of the contract, in 1941, the most promising black surgeon serving under him would be appointed to take his place. Apparently, Drew quickly was taken under Howes's wing, and deservedly so. On February 19, 1938, in a letter to Dr. Lambert of the GEB, Howes termed Drew a "good man, who taught well, showed good judgment, and had practically no race prejudice." It was not surprising, then, when Drew was selected, together with Dr. James R. Laurey, for advanced training in surgery—Drew at Columbia University and Laurey at the University of Michigan. Following Drew's death, Laurey would succeed him as chief of surgery. By 1942, after Drew had returned to Howard to teach, there were one hundred physicians making up the medical school faculty. Thirty-four, like Drew, were full-time; eighteen, with Drew among them, were former GEB fellows of one kind or another; and all but a couple of these fellows were among the full-time faculty.

Howard University and its medical school may be said to be the children of Civil War and Reconstruction Era liberalism; both were kept alive, though sometimes barely, by the largesse of the federal government. But just as assuredly—since the university itself re-

ceived GEB support, too, including $450,000 in 1929 for land ac-
quisition for future expansion—both are also the product of wise,
judicious, and generous philanthropy, especially from the Rockefeller Foundation through the General Education Board.

NOTES

Aside from the more general information included here—information
that properly may be considered a part of the general, or public, domain—this chapter is based exclusively upon General Education Board
archival material. This material mostly consists of correspondence between the GEB and Howard University Medical School officials, found in
the records of the General Education Board, located at the Rockefeller
Archive Center, North Tarrytown, New York, in Folders 255–273 and
7220.

5

To Howard, and on to Columbia

Drew was thirty-one years old when he arrived at Howard University in 1935. Ahead of him were his surgical residency at Howard, two more years of study at Presbyterian Hospital and at Columbia University, all of his famed research and work in fluid balance, banked blood, and blood plasma, and finally, his own distinguished career as surgeon and trainer of other surgeons. These years also included marriage and raising four children. But in all, Drew would have barely fifteen years in which to do these things, before, at the very peak of his accomplishment, his life would be tragically cut short.

Drew's initial appointment to Howard, for the 1935–36 year, was as an instructor in pathology, a more or less routine course for young surgeons. The following year, 1936–37, he was made assistant in surgery at the medical school and resident in surgery at Freedmen's Hospital. For the 1937–38 year, he moved up to instructor in surgery on the medical school faculty and assistant surgeon at the hospital. By then it was clear to all, including Dr. Edward L. Howes—the white surgeon on loan to Howard from Yale under the General Education Board grant and the chief surgeon at the hospital whom Drew was training under—that Drew clearly was one of Dean Adams's brightest stars. So, as the previous chapter noted, Howes recommended him to Adams for one of the first two-year fellowships for advanced training. For Drew, this meant Columbia University in New York City and its affiliated Presbyterian Hospital.

The Department of Surgery at Columbia was headed by Dr. Allen O. Whipple, and he assigned Drew to work under Dr. John Scudder, assistant professor of clinical surgery. At that time Scudder was directing research in the areas of fluid balance, especially during surgery, and blood chemistry and blood transfusion. Drew's interests in these areas went back to his student days at McGill, so it was a near-ideal assignment. But there was also the matter of his surgical training—midway through his first year at Columbia-Presbyterian a vacancy occurred among the residents, and Drew received an appointment as a full-fledged member of the resident staff, which, of course, included teaching duties. For the next year and a half, the remainder of the period of the fellowship, Drew was thus a surgical resident at one of the nation's leading research and teaching hospitals.

The surgical skills that he honed there were to be the dominant factor in the rest of his professional life, at least when it came to the task of passing them on to others in Howard's own surgical resident training program. Although the public would remember Drew for his work with blood plasma transfusion, his colleagues and students, including his surgical residents at Howard, would remember him chiefly as a great surgeon and great teacher of surgeons. As for Drew himself, he would come to say of his role in the development of blood plasma transfusion, that (along with football) it was one of the two things he was trying to live down.

But from 1938 to 1940, blood research was at the heart of the reputation he had to live *up* to if he were to receive the coveted Doctor of Science in Medicine degree. In time he would present to his major professor, Dr. Whipple, the result of that research in a doctoral dissertation titled "Banked Blood." Legend has it that the first version he showed Dr. Whipple was "New York telephone directory in size," so that Whipple returned it with the notation, "Too long," and the admonition, "Cut it down." [1]

The long and not very glorious history of blood transfusion before World War II probably would have led inevitably to just such a study as Drew's "Banked Blood," for without a viable means of blood storage, blood transfusion probably would never have become more than a medical curiosity. But in 1938, Scudder and

Drew were true pioneers, not only in the field of blood transfusion and blood preservation, but, in a sense, in the larger field of transplantation itself. Thus, in order to place Drew and his work in meaningful perspective, it is first necessary to look at the problems he and Scudder faced and the progress that others had already made toward solving those problems.

The transplantation of human organs has long intrigued the world of medicine, for after the body dies its organs and tissues may continue to "live" for some time after. As medical science has demonstrated with transplants of corneas, hearts, heart and lungs, kidneys, pancreases, and livers, sometimes organs may be transplanted from a dead body to a living one. Transplants of corneas and kidneys have proven especially successful. Drew himself once carefully wrote that "death is only the moment of dissolution of an intricate complex of mutual relations between the separate tissues of an organism, which individually retain their vitality for a varying time after the organism as a whole has ceased to function."[2]

Blood, too, in a sense, can be viewed in this same light. However, it has this additional and unique advantage: it is able to be transfused from a live body to another (not just from a dead body), and, within limitations, the donor's body will be able to replace or regenerate the lost blood within a few weeks at most. Hence, it is not surprising that blood transfusion was successfully practiced long before organ transplantation—a more recent phenomenon, especially in the case of heart, heart-lung, and liver transplants.

Probably the first successful transfusion of blood (but between animals only) was carried out by the English physiologist Richard Lower in the year 1665. Two years later, in 1667, in France, the first well-documented transfusion of blood into a human was carried out by Jean Baptiste Denis, but the blood of a lamb was used. Not surprisingly, the patient died. At this time, blood transfusion was largely a novelty and not a procedure of great promise, though there were great expectations for it, perhaps premature. At any rate, not until 1818 did James Blundell, the English physiologist and obstetrician, revive the procedure and start to advocate it, especially in cases of acute hemorrhage. But unlike the investigators of the seventeenth century, Blundell insisted upon the use of human, not animal, blood. Despite this breakthrough, however, more than fifty years later, in 1875, there were documented records of only 347 transfusions having been performed worldwide.

This record is understandable though, for the procedure was crude and difficult. It was performed either vein to vein through a tube, or by syringe into the recipient patient after the blood was drawn from the donor. When the tube method was used, there was, of course, no way to measure the amount transfused, though later on, frequent hemoglobin counts from the recipient were used to get a rough measure. Also there was always the risk of infection to both donor and recipient from nonsterile needles and other equipment, as well as the danger of malaria, syphilis, or infectious hepatitis being transmitted to the recipient. In addition, until after 1900, when Karl Landsteiner announced the discovery of the three basic blood groupings or types, A, B, and AB (the fourth, type O, was added in 1902), there was the danger of serious complications, or even death, due to blood type incompatibility. The whole business was tricky and dangerous and always further complicated by the need to have a donor right at hand. Obviously what was needed was some means of storing the blood of donors until needed—a "blood bank," at it came to be called (just as today the ideal would be a supply of human spare parts, or organs, such as corneas, kidneys, livers, and hearts, for example, ready to be taken out of storage and set to work saving the life of a new owner's body).

Thus it was that in 1835 T. L. W. Bischoff, a German, was the first to use preserved, or stored, blood. But it was not whole blood that Bischoff used; it had been defibrinated—that is, the essential clotting factor, fibrin, had been removed, leaving what is known as blood serum. (Today, of course, instead of removing the fibrin, an anticoagulant is added to whole blood that is not going to be used immediately.) Over the next forty years, at least three other investigators repeated the Bischoff procedure, while in 1914 A. Hustin of Belgium published the results of his experiments in the preservation of blood by the addition of the anticoagulant sodium citrate. The next year, 1915, Dr. R. Weil, of Memorial Hospital in New York, demonstrated that blood preserved in this manner could be kept for three to five days without deteriorating or endangering the life of the recipient when transfused. Another American, Dr. O. H. Robertson, while serving with the French army in 1917, managed to establish a blood bank of sorts even under battlefield conditions, but it was a bank of "modified blood," produced by aspirating off the plasma (which is the liquid part of whole fresh blood) and suspending the red cells in gelatin. Both were then refrigerated, to be reconstituted as modified blood when needed. Unfortunately, after some twenty-two successful and beneficial transfusions, the Germans overran that sector of the front, and the experiment was ended.

Russian scientists, however, deserve the real credit for fostering and advancing the idea of a true blood bank. They worked with cadaver blood (that is, blood from the dead). This line of research was sparked in 1927 by V. N. Shamov. He theorized that blood could be taken from a fresh cadaver and used for transfusion into a living body, so long as it was of the proper type. In 1930, S. S. Yudin, another Russian, did just that, with the first successful transfusion of cadaver blood, which was three days old. The patient recovered, more successful trials followed, and by 1932 Yudin had done one hundred such transfusions. By 1938 he had done twenty-five hundred, with only seven deaths and a reaction rate of just 5 percent. Yudin recommended that cadaver blood be used within ten days of its collection, since older blood tended to lead to jaundice in the recipient. Meanwhile, other Russian physicians continued the same line of research and treatment, but none as successfully as Yudin.

In a highly technical, though lucid and well-written, professional paper on Soviet contributions to blood transfusion research prepared for the *American Review of Soviet Medicine,* Drew wrote in 1944 that to the Russians "must go the credit for supplying the early work, most of the fundamental knowledge, and the impetus which has to a large degree been responsible for the widespread creation of the blood and plasma banks. . . ."[3]

Even when banked, however, whole blood has the disadvantage of a relatively short shelf life (until quite recently, only about four weeks, unless frozen, though the maximum is now about five weeks). In modern hospitals this limitation is acceptable, even though it often leads to the waste of blood, but it is not acceptable in many other cases, such as in isolated rural areas and on the battlefield, for example. In these cases, until a true blood substitute, or artificial blood, is developed—and several kinds are now in the experimental stage—blood plasma will remain the only choice whenever a transfusion is needed.

Energetic, dedicated, and devoted to both his research and his surgical training, Drew kept long hours and what many would regard as a killing pace, though it was perhaps not too different from the routine followed by thousands of surgical residents before him, and thousands more since. It should be pointed out in Drew's favor, however, that most surgical residents do not simultaneously pursue an advanced degree in medicine.

Even so, Drew found time—though barely—to court and to marry while he was at Columbia. This event, of course, changed the whole mode of his personal life, but it seems to have in no way changed the professional path he had marked out for himself. It did, however, give him a chance to confront himself in verbal fashion and to reveal himself as he never had before (except, perhaps, for that dreary, lonely, and poverty-ridden New Year's Day in Montreal in 1930, when he bared his soul on paper, producing the soliloquy recounted in chapter 3). Courtship and marriage revealed Drew for the first time—at least to those who study his life from the written record he left behind—to be an inveterate letter-writer, a romantic, a dreamer, and a planner, who knew both where he was going and how to get there. His correspondence with his wife, before and after their marriage, and then with a few other individuals in later years, also revealed Drew to be a considerable man of letters—and while he could "lay on the romance" heavily, he could also clearly and movingly define his dreams and goals.

NOTES

1. David Hepburn, "The Life of Dr. Charles R. Drew," *Our World* (July, 1950): 25.

2. Charles Richard Drew, "The Role of Soviet Investigators in the Development of the Blood Bank," *American Review of Soviet Medicine*, 1 (Apr., 1944): 360.

3. Ibid., 368.

W. Montague Cobb, "Charles Richard Drew, M.D., 1904–1950," *Journal of the National Medical Association*, 42 (July, 1950): 239–242; Hepburn, "The Life of Dr. Charles R. Drew," 25; Charles R. Drew, "Banked Blood" (Ph.D. diss., Columbia University, 1940); Albert R. Lamb, *The Presbyterian Hospital and the Columbia-Presbyterian Medical Center, 1868–1943: A History of a Great Medical Adventure* (New York: Columbia University Press, 1955), 371–72; Drew, "The Role of Soviet Investigators in the Development of the Blood Bank," 360, 363, 368.

6

"Dear Lenore" I

Typically for Drew, even when it came to finding a wife he was in the midst of his pursuit of medicine—he found her while on his way to a professional meeting.

It was in the early spring of 1939, Drew's first year in New York. He had received an invitation to participate in the annual clinic at the John A. Andrew Memorial Hospital in Tuskegee, Alabama (the same one that he was en route to eleven years later when he was fatally injured). The clinic gave him a chance to get out of New York and visit with some of his Howard University colleagues. After first spending a day with his family in Arlington, Virginia, he and three other Howard University physicians set out for Tuskegee by automobile. They stopped in Atlanta to visit friends, and it was there that he met Minnie Lenore Robbins, a young instructor of home economics at Spelman College.

Lenore, then twenty-eight, was a native of Philadelphia and had attended Cheyney State College, in Cheyney, Pennsylvania; she later transferred to Spelman College, from which she graduated, and then stayed on to teach. Apparently she and Drew were smitten with one another at first sight, though Drew was more spellbound than Lenore. At any rate, as soon as the clinic in Alabama was over, Drew left his companions and returned by a train that made a stopover in Atlanta. There, only three days after their first meeting, Drew went to visit Lenore at her dormitory at about 1:00 in the morning, awoke the matron in charge, and insisted upon seeing Lenore. Surprised, naturally, she came down to talk to him, but he had more on his mind than talk—he proposed! Lenore at least halfway accepted; if all continued to go well, they would marry sometime that fall.

Theirs did not prove to be a match made in heaven, but it was a natural one of two extraordinary people. Dr. Asa G. Yancey, a native of Atlanta and later one of Drew's surgical residents (who went on to become medical director of Atlanta's Grady Memorial Hospital and associate dean of the Emory University School of Medicine) knew Lenore when she was a student at Spelman. More than forty years later he recalled how she was one of the most striking, vivacious, and beautiful girls on the campus.

Drew, as we know, was a handsome man, and he delighted in female company. In fact, he was one of those men who just naturally attracted women; it was a trait that he enjoyed, and it was one that he made the most of—which does not mean that he was a Casanova plying a Casanova's trade, or that he ever was involved with anyone else's wife. Like H. L. Mencken, Drew probably found women to be "the incomparable buzz-saw" of life, possessed of the same allurement for men "that Cape Hatteras holds for sailors."[1]

Drew wrote to Lenore almost immediately, even before he got back to New York, penning the first of the many letters he would write to her during the course of his life. The letters sometimes were short and boyishly gushy; at other times they were long, wandering, and frankly didactic, as if he were seeking to dominate her intellectually; or they might contain a lengthy quotation from some favorite poem, or even an original poem. Sometimes Drew's letters were just long, almost in a stream-of-consciousness style; at those times he laid his soul bare. At still other times, in no uncertain terms, he could display the wrath of his displeasure.

One of the earliest letters was written on April 9, 1939, in Washington, D.C., just after Drew returned from that first meeting with, and proposal to, Lenore. With an almost sacred yet romantic style, he dated the letter with exactitude: "Easter Sunday, at Twilight. Since first seeing you," he wrote, "I have moved through the days as one in a dream, lost in revery, awed by the speed with which the moving finger of fate has pointed out the way I should go." Then, almost as if he were admitting that for now, at least, he saw her and all the world through rose-colored glasses, he wrote:

"Later, when I become coherent, I shall perhaps see many things, but tonight this one thing alone seems to ring clearly—I love you." The letter was signed "Charlie." [2]

Four days later, on April 13, 1939, writing from New York at 3:00 in the morning, Drew remembered to describe to Lenore something he had witnessed the afternoon of that Easter Sunday he had first written to her. It was a concert given by Marian Anderson at the Lincoln Memorial in Washington, D.C., held there after the Daughters of the American Revolution had withdrawn an invitation for her to sing in Constitution Hall because she was a Negro. Following an explosion of indignation from black leaders and liberal whites, Secretary of the Interior, Harold Ickes, "the old curmudgeon," invited her to sing in the presence of the statue of the Great Emancipator.

> Sunday afternoon I went down to the Lincoln Memorial to hear Marian Anderson sing. In all my life I have never seen such an impressive thing. With the soft rays of a pink sun gleaming against the white marble beauty of that magnificent structure and reflecting itself in the long still pool of water that stretches off toward the Washington Monument, she raised her exquisite voice in song and lifted with a sweep of melody a whole race to higher levels of thought, feeling, and hope. Countless thousands paid her tribute of almost reverent silence when she sang her songs of joy and sorrow. She held them beneath her magic sway, making them laugh or sigh at will, and when she finished with "Nobody knows de trouble I've seen," many eyes were moist with unashamed tears and hearts too full for words. [3]

The Sunday following the Marian Anderson concert, at 2:00 in the morning, Drew wrote Lenore about how, for years, he not only had worked, planned, and dreamed of becoming "a good doctor, and able surgeon," but "in my wildest moments perhaps also playing some part in establishing a real school of thought among Negro physicians and guiding younger fellows to levels of accomplishments not yet attained by any of us." Romance soon crept into the same letter, however, as it ended with a quotation of Elizabeth Barrett Browning's poem "How Do I Love Thee" in its entirety. [4]

Clearly, Drew was the more romantic of the two, for on May 3, 1939, we find him writing, concerned that he had said something "wrong"—something which had caused Lenore to write, "Frankly,

I'm not sure a wife would help you." He assured her that his desire
was not "just to have a woman—the streets are full of them, the
drawing rooms too"—it had to be Lenore. Then, as if he were bait-
ing her, he wrote: "Really, I think I have possibilities if someone
like you took the raw material in hand." But Drew was still worried, for Lenore had ignored his request to tell him about her
dreams, when a little girl, of the kind of husband, the kind of house
she wanted when she married. "Then you next said you didn't see
how you could help. I almost dread your next letter, but I'll wait
it with trembling knees." [5]

Two weeks later Drew wrote, begging her to reconsider her decision not to visit him in New York after she had first promised to
come. "Things are not as dark perhaps as the tone of my letters
would indicate at times. It is simply that I would rather promise
little and fulfill all that I promise—than promise much out of the
pure exuberance of days like these and find later that my deeds
fell short of my words." [6] His pleading worked, for the next week
he wrote how he was glad that "you changed your mind," and that
he would take Lenore to the World's Fair while she was in New
York. [7]

Sometime in late May in an undated letter, he proudly wrote
how Dr. Whipple had allowed him to register for the degree of
Doctor of Science in Medicine. "There are no such Negroes at present [that is, with such a degree. Dr. Robert A.] Lambert of the
Rockefeller Foundation is opposed to it, attempts have been made
by others to no avail." But, he wrote, "It's much more than a degree
I'm after. There are those in high places who feel that Negroes have
not yet reached intellectual levels which will permit their attempting the very highest reaches."

Lenore was planning a visit to Washington to meet Drew's family, and he wrote in that same letter that his sister Nora, Mrs. Francis Gregory, would meet her at the train. "I'd like to have you see
the rest of the Drews. Each Sunday at four they eat together. They
consist of Joe, my brother, usually not too bad, but mean as a bull
now since he's laid up with a broken leg [he had fallen off the roof]
. . . unable to work and likely to go in debt during the summer.
Well, I guess he's got a right to be blue." Then, there was "Grace,
his wife—never says much [but] knows a lot . . . and really is a
swell person." Joe and Grace, he said, had two boys, aged six and

three. Nora was pregnant, while "Eva, my kid sister, has just reached the jitterbug stage [and is] a senior in high school. You see, I think they're pretty swell. I'm the prodigal, the wanderer, the black sheep of the family. Yet, strange enough, I fear a bit of the pet because I'm never there." And then this: "The whole thing revolves, of course, around my mother."[8]

Drew's next letter, on June 16, 1939, was almost steamingly sensuous, yet proper. He compared Lenore—"chaste, cool, no cuddling, no surreptitious movements, no guile or knowing glance in your eyes"—to Lorraine, a married woman, who was "soft, cuddling, almost voluptuous," in a discreet sort of way. "I like it [Lorraine's way] can't help it, so my reaction in the case of somebody's wife" is, "This is no place for me." Then the confident, bantering Drew wrote to his intended: "Together our offspring will have two hurdles to jump at birth—gigantism and genius—most parents face worse."[9]

Before the month was out, in a complete change of pace, Drew wrote on June 25 that he had just come from an all-Wagner concert. "I like it, but to say that I was carried away would be affectation. Nothing in my background makes Wagner dear to me. I did not hear it when I was small . . . except for 'Tannhauser,' which my father used to sing."[10]

The next week Drew wrote on July 3 that he had been to see a ballet troupe at Lewisohn Stadium, where the role of Sylphides was danced to the music of Chopin. But on Wednesday night he saw Joe Louis in a title bout with the New Jersey heavyweight Tony Galento. It "looked a little rocky" for Louis in the first round, and again in the third, he wrote. But when Louis "really got going in the fourth it was something to behold."

> He is certainly a grand athlete, beautiful in action and a terrific puncher. Galento, at the end, just sort of walked away in a daze and slid down the referee's legs, a badly beaten, cut-up, clumsy-looking, little fat man. When he came to he acted as one with no breeding either as a gentleman or an athlete usually acts. Joe Louis, in spite of his reputedly low I.Q., has yet to act other than a true thoroughbred.

That letter was a potpourri, and one in which Drew lapsed into a sort of everyday vernacular as he related how a black group known as "The New Englanders," gave "their annual bust out . . . a gala affair, held downtown in one of the nicer hotels [where] our folks really put on the dog and they did look good. That group, I suppose, is just about the best looking bunch of young ladies of color that I know of. But," he wrote, "I didn't even flirt once—that's pretty good for me. I wish you had been there." Then Drew jumped to the news that sister Nora had suffered a miscarriage. And finally he closed by writing: "A full clear moon tonight shines over the water of the Hudson and way below the faint noises of the city streets go on and on in a sort of obligato. . . ."[11]

Drew and Lenore were married on September 23, 1939, and settled into a small $100-a-month apartment in New York located at 250 West 150th Street, which they shared with another couple. Lenore obtained a laboratory job as one of Drew's assistants, while Drew went back to his research on blood preservation, his surgical work, and his patients.

NOTES

1. H. L. Mencken, "The Incomparable Buzz-Saw," *Smart Set,* (May, 1919).

2. Drew to Lenore, April 9, 1939, CRD Papers. The letters cited in the rest of the notes for this chapter are also from the CRD Papers.

3. Drew to Lenore, April 13, 1939.

4. Drew to Lenore, April 16, 1939.

5. Drew to Lenore, May 3, 1939.

6. Drew to Lenore, May 17, 1939.

7. Drew to Lenore, May 23, 1939.

8. Drew to Lenore, n.d., "Sunday morning."

9. Drew to Lenore, June 16, 1939.

10. Drew to Lenore, June 25, 1939.

11. Drew to Lenore, July 3, 1939.

Lenore Robbins Drew, "Unforgettable Charlie Drew," *Reader's Digest* (Mar., 1978): 136–37; interview with Dr. Asa G. Yancey.

7

Blood for Britain:
Fame and Myth Come

The research of Scudder and Drew first centered on the preservation of whole blood, not on the production of blood plasma; that research focus came later, at or about the time that Drew finished his dissertation, "Banked Blood," in April 1940. But in order to write a scientific treatise on the preservation and storage of whole blood, it was necessary, indeed inevitable, that Scudder and his assistant, Drew, develop their own blood bank at Presbyterian Hospital.

The first facility in the United States for the storage of whole blood was at Cook County Hospital in Chicago. It was established by Dr. Bernard Fantus in March 1937, and it was he who coined the quickly adopted term, "blood bank." By that time numerous similar blood banks were already in operation in the Soviet Union, however.

In 1937 at about the same time, Dr. Scudder began his research at the Columbia-Presbyterian Medical Center with a grant from the Trubee Foundation. In 1938 he received an additional two-year Commonwealth Fellowship to continue his work. It was then that Drew joined him. Scudder later called Drew not only "my most brilliant student, but one of the greatest clinical scientists of the first half of the twentieth century."[1]

On August 9, 1939, near the end of Drew's first year in New York and just before his marriage, Presbyterian's own experimental blood bank opened. Scudder and Drew were virtual unknowns in

a field in which only several other American specialists had published, in contrast to the Soviet Union, where use of stored blood
was common.

Such is the usual course of science. Rarely are great advances in
scientific knowledge the work of just one man or one woman toil-
ing away in a laboratory. So, in truth, what Drew accomplished in
"Banked Blood" was to bring together not only the results of his
own research and the knowledge gained through the Presbyterian
Hospital's blood bank, but all that was known on the subject at
that time, whatever the source of that knowledge. Dr. Scudder, ten
years after Drew's death, said that "Banked Blood" was considered
a masterpiece. Strangely, however, it was never published.

In June 1940, Columbia University conferred the degree Doctor
of Science in Medicine upon Drew, in recognition of his dissertation. As the first black recipient of that degree, Drew prepared to
return to Howard University to what he hoped would be his life's
work of training other young black surgeons. For himself, and for
Howard, his dreams were large, as he spelled them out to a friend,
Edwin B. Henderson:

> My work here is about finished. I've gone as far as I can go in formal
> medicine, so I guess I'll have to go to work now. It has been good
> fun. Chiefly, I suppose, because it [receipt of the Doctor of Science
> in Medicine degree by a Negro] has never been done before and it
> is felt that the higher reaches of medicine are not for him. On Tues-
> day, I get the degree Doctor of Science in Medicine. Now that all is
> over but the shouting, it feels about like the day after a big race is
> won. . . . The only thing in medicine is that it takes so much longer.
> When it is all over, it is just another medal in the box and we begin
> looking forward to next season's competition. My next big "meet"
> is at Howard in the Department of Surgery. . . . [For] seventy years
> there has been a Howard Medical School but still there is no tradi-
> tion; no able surgeon has ever been trained there; no school of
> thought has been born there; few of their stars have ever hit the
> headlines. In American surgery, there are no Negro representatives;
> in so far as the men who count know, all Negro doctors are just
> country practitioners, capable of sitting with the poor and the sick
> of their race but not given to too much intellectual activity and not
> particularly interested in advancing medicine. This attitude I should
> like to change. It should be great sport.[2]

Following his graduation in June 1940, Drew returned to Howard with a promotion. When he had left two years earlier, his appointment had been as instructor in surgery at Howard and assistant surgeon at Freedmen's Hospital. Now he would be an assistant professor in surgery at Howard and a surgeon at Freedmen's. But just three months later he was back in New York, on leave. Although only six months would mark his absence from Howard— late September 1940 to late March 1941—they were to prove an important six months, not only because of what he would accomplish in that brief space, but also because he would begin to be swallowed up in much of the myth that still surrounds the name Charles R. Drew.

World War II came to Europe in September 1939 and burst into a blitzkrieg in the spring of 1940 with the return of good weather. As the number of casualties soared, so did the need for blood transfusions, but maintaining blood banks in cities under aerial attack and blood banks at or near the actual battlefront just was not feasible. In answer to this need, another line of blood research entered the picture—blood plasma.

Simply stated, plasma is the pale yellow or gray-yellow protein-containing, fluid portion of the blood in which the red corpuscles are normally suspended. Remove these red cells—the part of whole blood that readily deteriorates—and what is left, now called blood plasma, is a convenient and storable fluid expander, but not a true blood substitute, since plasma does not carry oxygen. Carrying oxygen is a function of the red cells, which are not present in blood plasma. However, blood plasma is especially useful when there has been a great loss of blood, or when, as in the case of burns, there is a continuing loss of fluid and blood protein. It is also very useful, and for a long time was even the treatment of choice, in many cases of severe trauma, or shock.

The advantages of blood plasma, even though it is not a true blood substitute, are impressive: it can be produced at comparatively little expense; it can be stored for long periods without risk of deterioration; no blood typing is necessary since it contains no red cells (the typeable portion of whole blood); and there is little or no danger of serious reaction, even after repeated and large transfusions. Finally, whether plasma is in liquid, frozen, or dried form (the most common form), it rarely transmits syphilis or malaria during transfusion, something that more readily happens with whole blood. This danger is only possible when liquid blood plasma is used (the first form of plasma developed, which soon became outmoded). Anyway, the danger can be avoided completely if the blood used to make liquid plasma is first stored for about seven days. Transmission of infectious hepatitis is a danger, however, with all three forms of plasma, and careful donor selection is the only preventive.

Of course, these dangers were not fully known in the summer of 1940, but already, by the time Drew completed his dissertation, his and Scudder's research was pointing more and more toward blood plasma. World War II was a catalyst that speeded up research in that direction. And it is with blood plasma research that the Drew myth begins to appear.

The fact is, Drew did not develop blood plasma in any of its forms, nor did he perfect blood transfusion with blood plasma, as is sometimes claimed in newspapers and popular magazines, in children's books, on television, and even in some history books. It is especially worth noting that no recognized and respected medical or scientific authority or publication has ever made such claims for Drew. Certainly, Drew did not make any such claims for himself, nor have any of his former colleagues or any of his students. To say all this, however, in no way detracts from Drew's actual accomplishments, which well may appear greater if allowed to stand in their own light.

Why all the misleading stories, then? In large part they are the result of the general public's ignorance or misunderstanding of how great scientific advances are made. Much of the public—romantically and idealistically—wants to believe that within science, and medicine especially, there are George Washingtons and Abraham Lincolns who either "founded" or "saved" the health of the republic. Put another way, perhaps those same members of the public find it easier to believe, or prefer to believe, the creation story, for miracle though it is, it is easier to grasp than the idea of evolution. Still others—some blacks and some white liberals—are simply looking for the "super Negro" to place upon a pedestal. Whatever the reason, truth (and ultimately even Drew himself) must be the loser, if the myth continues to be perpetuated.

Long before development of the first successful blood banks anywhere, military physicians began searching for some feasible way to administer transfusions under battlefield conditions. In 1918, Captain Gordon R. Ward, an English physician, first suggested that blood plasma alone be used instead of whole blood, but it was an American, Dr. John R. Elliott, and his associates (of Salisbury, North Carolina), who led the research into the substitution of blood plasma for whole blood. Dr. Elliott first made his findings public in the paper, "A Preliminary Report of a New Method of Blood Transfusion," which he read before a regional medical meeting in Salisbury on September 24, 1936. Three months later, in the December issue of *Southern Medicine and Surgery,* the paper was published. Dr. Elliott continued his research, and in December 1939, *Military Surgeon* published another of his papers on the subject, as did the *North Carolina Medical Journal* in June 1940, and the *Journal of the American Medical Association* in September 1940.

All of Dr. Elliott's work was with liquid plasma, but from the surgeon general of the United States down, military physicians were still looking for and hoping for a dried version of plasma that readily could be reconstituted. However, that research, too, was already well under way: for example, in the November 1935 issue of the *Journal of Immunology,* Doctors Stuart Mudd and Eliot M. Flosdorf of Philadelphia described a process for drying plasma. At Sharp and Dohme Laboratories of Philadelphia, Doctors William J. Elser and John Reichel were also at work on dried plasma, and in 1938 Dr. Max Strumia of Philadelphia's Bryn Mawr Hospital began actual production, in very small amounts, of dried plasma, using a drying unit that he had developed himself. By 1940 Scudder and Drew were also experimenting with plasma—not dried plasma, however, but liquid plasma that they had obtained from Dr. Elliott in North Carolina. The actual clinical testing was carried out by Drew at Presybterian Hospital.

At that time, shortly before the collapse of France, reports were coming from Europe of the usefulness of plasma and the great need for it. Thus it was that on June 12, 1940, at a special meeting of the Board of Trustees and the Board of Medical Control of the Blood Tranfusion Betterment Association held at the New York Academy of Medicine, that a "Blood for Britain" program was approved, contingent upon the cooperation, including financial support, of the American Red Cross. Indeed, without that cooperation and support the program, in all probability, would never have gotten off the ground. Also attending the meeting were representatives of the National Research Council, several commercial laboratories, and the army surgeon general's office and also a number of scientists engaged in blood preservation research, including plasma. Both Scudder and Drew were there as well, by invitation.

At subsequent meetings of the Blood Transfusion Betterment Association, held in July, August, and September 1940, the Blood for Britain (actually blood *plasma*) program was organized. In all there were eleven such meetings, but Drew was present only at the meeting of July 12. After that he was back at Howard University.

Technical direction of the program was handled by Scudder and Dr. C. P. Rhoads of Memorial Hospital in New York. At the meeting of August 5, Scudder was offered the position of medical supervisor of the program, which he declined because of commitments to Columbia University and Presbyterian Hospital. In anticipation of Scudder's response, a letter had been simultaneously sent to Drew asking if he would be available for the position. He replied, "Yes," and thus soon became supervisor.

The first trial shipment of plasma left New York by air on August 9 by way of the United States embassy in Lisbon, Portugal, and two weeks later the British sent word that it was "entirely satisfactory." On August 15, the Blood for Britain program was officially inaugurated at Presbyterian Hospital. Soon eight other hospitals in the New York metropolitan area joined the program, and soon, too, problems began to appear. Many of the bottles of plasma arrived with a cloudy appearance. It was known that if the donor ate a hearty meal an hour or so before donating blood that the plasma would be cloudy, and in that case it was harmless. But cloudiness could also be due to contamination, and since the British could not, under wartime conditions, be expected to test every bottle for purity, the Board of Medical Control on September 13 requested that donors be instructed not to eat for four hours before giving blood. In the very first days of the program, that had been the recommended policy, but it had been rescinded out of fear that the additional inconvenience might discourage would-be donors.

At the same meeting it was also stipulated that all tests for sterility control established under regulations of the United States Public Health Service should thereafter be complied with.

Thus the major technical problems of the Blood for Britain project had been solved by the time that the Board of Medical Control, on September 20, created the position of "full-time medical supervisor to act as liaison officer between the board and the hospital engaged in procuring plasma for shipment to the British Red Cross," and offered it to Drew. Howard University granted him a four-month leave of absence, and in late September Drew arrived in New York to undertake his duties as medical supervisor.

In the story of Drew's involvement with the Blood for Britain program, there is the matter of a troublesome, if legitimate, telegram, which, when cited out of historical context, gives a false impression of the magnitude of Drew's role in the program. Dr. John Beattie, chief of the transfusion service for the Royal Air Force and one of Drew's old teachers at McGill—the one who helped interest him in blood preservation research—cabled on September 3, while Drew was still at Howard (almost a month before he joined the Blood for Britain program in New York): "Could you secure five thousand ampoules dried plasma for transfusion work immediately and follow this by equal quantity in three to four weeks? Contents each ampoule should represent about one pint whole plasma."[3] Of course, Drew could not. Not only was there not that much dried plasma in the whole world at that time, but Drew was not even a part of the program for collecting it.

Beattie may have been playing a foxy game, however, trying to get his old pupil, and the physician he felt best qualified, into a position that would help Britain and do honor to Drew, for at the same time he wired the Blood Transfusion Betterment Association: "Uniform standards for all blood banks of utmost importance. Suggest you appoint overall director if program is to continue. Suggest Charles R. Drew if available."[4] However, Beattie obviously did not know that a month earlier, on August 5, the Blood Transfusion Betterment Association had asked Drew if he would accept such a position, if it were offered. But perhaps Beattie's telegram to the Association did play some slight role in Drew's receiving the appointment.

Also, in another important development that occurred *before*

Drew assumed the position of medical supervisor, the Board of Medical Control ordered that its own blood research program increasingly move into the area of dried plasma, since the technology for it rapidly was becoming available, though too late to provide dried instead of liquid plasma to Britain. What *was* missing, until Drew arrived, were uniform procedures and standards for the collection of blood and the processing of blood plasma by the various participating hospitals. By that time Drew knew as much as anyone in the world about the preservation of whole blood, and he had kept on top of the growing body of literature on blood plasma and had conducted clinical trials with it at Presbyterian Hospital. He was thus an ideal choice for medical supervisor of the Blood for Britain program. He was also a perfectionist who thrived on doing things right and having others do them right. Another asset was his natural flair for organization that now came to the fore, as it had earlier when he coached athletics, and as it would later when he headed the Department of Surgery at Howard. Add to this his commanding presence and capacity for quelling discord, and the Blood Transfusion Betterment Association had found in one man everything needed, and more, to fill a post that called for organizational skills and diplomacy as well as technical expertise.

It was no wonder, then, that before even two weeks had passed with Drew as medical supervisor, he was both making his presence felt and gaining recognition. For instance, the Medical Review Board quickly adopted his recommendation that, in the interests of rigorous quality control, all plasma collected should undergo final processing in one central laboratory. The national U.S. blood program that followed the Blood for Britain project also adopted that policy. The idea of mobile blood collecting units with refrigeration facilities was another of Drew's innovations. Today, of course, they are one of the most visible signs of continuing blood collection. Largely to Drew's credit, before the month of October was out Great Britain was receiving plasma that was uniformly sterile.

Meanwhile, it had always been understood, both in Great Britain and in the United States, that the Blood for Britain program was a temporary expedient, intended to exist only until Britain could develop its own plasma program. In late October, with four processing centers already operating in the London area and more on the way, the Blood Transfusion Betterment Association was notified that after January 1941, American plasma no longer would be needed. By that date, though, it was becoming increasingly apparent that in the interest of national defense, the United States should plan for a national blood collection program of its own. Once that decision was made, it became equally obvious that Drew's knowledge, skills, and experience would be needed even more than they had been in the Blood for Britain program, which had embraced only the New York City area. So before his leave of absence from Howard expired at the end of January 1941, Drew requested an extension, and a three-month one was granted.

NOTES

1. American Red Cross, *Dr. Charles Drew, Medical Pioneer* (pamphlet, dated Nov., 1970).

2. Drew to Edwin B. Henderson, May 31, 1940, CRD Papers.

3. John Beattie to Drew, September 3, 1940, ibid.

4. John Beattie to Blood Transfusion Betterment Association, September 3, 1940, copy in CRD Papers.

For much, if not most, of the material in this chapter and the next, the author is indebted to the late Clyde E. Buckingham, longtime historian and research analyst at the National Headquarters of the American Red Cross, Washington, D.C., and his "Dr. Charles Richard Drew," a typescript "in-house" manuscript of roughly fifty pages that long bore the notation "Confidential." Written in 1968, it was apparently given confidential classification because at that time—the civil rights-conscious and sometimes turbulent sixties—it simply was not a popular course of action, and perhaps not a very wise one as well, to attempt to demythologize any black national hero, no matter how fairly and accurately. Buckingham's manuscript is an eminently fair and objective piece of scholarship, but with the label "racist" already too frequently applied to the American Red Cross because of its longstanding (but now defunct) policy of segregating blood by race—a policy forced upon it by the armed forces—that organization simply could not afford publicly to demythologize the man who is *supposed* to have resigned from the national blood bank program because of the Red Cross's blood segregation policy.

Other sources used were: Charles R. Drew, "The Role of Soviet Investigators in the Development of the Blood Bank," *American Review of*

Soviet Medicine, 1 (Apr., 1944): 367–68; Albert R. Lamb, *The Presbyterian Hospital and the Columbia-Presbyterian Medical Center, 1868–1943: A History of Great Medical Adventure* (New York: Columbia University Press, 1955): 372–74; interview with Dr. Asa G. Yancey; "Dr. Charles R. Drew," *The McGill News,* 31 (Summer, 1950).

CHAPTER

8

"Black" Blood, "White" Blood, and Home to Howard

While it was good news in 1940 that Britain now could meet all her blood plasma needs without help from abroad, the Blood Transfusion Betterment Association was worried that the end had come too suddenly. This was so because, though humanitarianism and concern for Britain's future had been the primary motivations behind the establishment of the Blood for Britain project, Britain's desperate situation had also given medical science the opportunity to clinically test the effectiveness of blood plasma on the large scale that only a major war could make possible. It had also provided an opportunity to learn whether blood plasma produced on a test-tube scale could now be mass-produced. In the five months that the program had lasted a great deal had been learned about both. Just how much had been learned and what had transpired in the Blood for Britain program was described in a report issued on January 31, 1941, by the Association. The entire medical, or technical, section of the report was written by Drew, and it was that report that catapulted him into the very front ranks of blood plasma science.

Eighteen years after Drew's death, a Red Cross in-house report on Drew's contributions to blood plasma research and production gave what is perhaps the best and fairest summation yet of those contributions. Drew had, the report said,

> brought together, for the benefit of hematologists everywhere, the latest knowledge acquired by scientists working in several fields.

Included were the result of research studies and clinical tests of academic and commercial laboratories on both sides of the Atlantic and the experience and practical know-how gained in both English and American programs. He had shown exceptional ability in synthesizing the work of others—in selecting from a multiplicity of diverse and often contradictory findings those which had practical application to the problems at hand. He used the discoveries of numerous other scientists, organizing such data into a workable process, which made possible a major step forward toward the goal of mass production of blood supplies in the large quantities and in the form which could be used by the armed forces under conditions of modern warfare.[1]

Almost overnight—but only outside the medical and scientific community—Drew became the man responsible for the development of blood plasma for transfusions. Of course, he was not, and no one knew that better than he. Without the discoveries of literally dozens of often unnamed scientists, as well as famed ones, there would have been no report for Drew to write, no report to place him in both the national and the international limelight. On the other hand, it is equally true that had there been no Charles R. Drew to pull together and synthesize all those findings and then to make a blood collection and plasma production program work, thousands of lives would have been lost as the world waited for some other figure to emerge and accomplish the work done so magnificently by Drew.

Both common sense and the national defense demanded that the conclusion of the Blood for Britain program not also spell the end of the applied-science endeavor it represented, or that the services of Drew be lost to that endeavor. Clearly, too, liquid plasma—even though it had proved possible to produce in large quantities—was not the long-range answer to meeting battlefront needs (as opposed to those of bombed cities). Dried plasma capable of readily being reconstituted was the only answer. Although the Blood for Britain program had spurred increased dried plasma research, especially at New York City's Memorial Hospital, how to mass-produce dried plasma was another, as yet unsolved, problem.

In light of these problems, and the possible needs of the nation, Drew and Tracy Voorhees, legal advisor to the Blood Transfusion Betterment Association, drew up plans for a continuing three-month program (matching Drew's extended leave of absence from Howard) that would be "essentially an experiment in mass production." It was to be jointly sponsored by the Association, the National Research Council, and the Red Cross. The armed forces, too, joined in requesting that those national organizations undertake such a program. They agreed, and Drew was named assistant director—under Dr. C. P. Rhoads, who had been overall technical director of the Blood for Britain program, and under whom Drew had worked while there. Drew also was made director of the Red Cross blood bank in New York City. As assistant director of the national program, Drew was, in practice, medical director in charge of the collection of blood for use by the armed forces. As director of the city blood bank, he was on the payroll of the New York City chapter of the Red Cross (instead of the national organization).

The pilot unit of the national blood collection program got under way at Presbyterian Hospital, on February 4, 1941, but almost from the start—since the new program lacked the emergency conditions that had sparked the Blood for Britain program—donors were slow to come forward. Another problem was also present, as it had been during the Blood for Britain program, which would soon add to the myth surrounding Drew and his actions—namely, what to do about Negro donors.

In the Blood for Britain program blood was designated by race, as was the plasma made from it. Response to the *supposed* British national temper was the reason for this practice, and not prejudice per se. But when the U.S. national program began in the winter of 1941, the armed forces *stipulated* that only white donors were to be accepted—or, as often was said, only "white" blood was to be accepted. Since this program involved blood collected by Americans for *use* by Americans, prejudice, in all probability, did figure in this decision. After all, the armed forces of the United States in 1941 were rigidly segregated, and they remained so throughout the war and until late in the decade. Perhaps in a nation where the black population approximated only about 12 percent of the total, and where "liberal thinking" on both social and political issues was not exactly a hallmark of the high command structure of the armed forces, such a policy of segregation was not surprising.

As for black servicemen who did not wish to receive "white" plasma made from "white" blood (if they were in any condition to make decisions), black donors of whole blood of the proper type (A, B, AB, or O) would be found—if available, that is. In practice, that meant that wounded blacks generally would receive "white" plasma. This practice could be condoned, it seems, since "white" blood apparently could not "pollute" or "contaminate" that of a black recipient. In addition, of course, even if "black" blood were not labeled "inferior," still a white recipient just might not want "black" blood coursing in his veins[!]

It was all pretty incredible, especially since all but a tiny minority of the scientific community knew—from every laboratory test known for measuring the content and the qualities of human blood—that all blood from the species *homo sapiens* was "equal." The only difference is blood type, which does not differentiate between races. Imagine Drew's position: although he was the medical supervisor of both the Blood for Britain program and the later national U.S. program, and despite the fact that he was the scientist who knew as much or more about blood as anyone living—he was not himself eligible to be a donor because he was a Negro!

Of course, there were those in the scientific community who, though they *knew* that human blood was just human blood (regardless of race, national origin, or social position) still would not publicly *say* as much, for fear of public ridicule by those who believed—whether out of ignorance or prejudice—that there was a difference. Given the social milieu of 1941, few physicians (regardless of where they received their medical education) who served a largely Caucasian, blue-collar body of patients (whether they were mill workers in Porterdale, Georgia, or Lynn, Massachusetts, or auto assembly workers in Detroit) would have been willing to dispute the folk wisdom of these patients on the subject of "black" and "white" blood. And the same could be said of rural physicians, whether they served an Alabama county deep in the heart of the Black Belt or one smack-dab in the middle of Iowa.

There was another problem, one that was apparently all but ignored by both the high command of the armed forces and by the white 88 percent of the population—namely, the morale of the black 12 percent of that population, who, though American citizens, were not eligible to be blood donors, even to black recipients! In January 1942, after the United States entered World War II, and while blacks as well as whites were being killed in that war, the policy of excluding black donors was changed to one of segregating the blood received from black donors, and then using it to produce plasma for black recipients. That was progress, of a sort.

It should be pointed out, in all fairness, that segregation of blood by race was never truly a policy of the Red Cross; it was insisted upon by the armed forces. But for too long a time it remained unchanged. It just *might* have been changed during the war in response to Negro protest, but for a frightening unknown: what effect would the announcement of a new policy—one calling for the blood of all donors, without regard to race, to be indiscriminately mixed—have upon a large section of the white population? Would whites be so alienated that they would refuse to continue supporting the blood donor program? No one knew, and since it was a matter of life and death—for black as well as for white servicemen—the policy of segregation of donated blood stood throughout the war.

During the entire time that Drew was associated with the national program for collection of blood for the armed forces, the policy was not segregation of blood from Negro donors, but rather, exclusion of Negro donors. In private, it was a policy that Drew obviously condemned, not only because he knew there was no scientific basis for it, but also because it was an insult to him personally and to the entire Negro race. Publicly, however, he was in no position to condemn the policy forced upon his employer, the New York City chapter of the Red Cross, by the armed forces of the United States.

Nevertheless, legend has it that Drew called a press conference for 2:00 in the afternoon, but without specifying a date (according to one author). There, speaking as a scientist and not as a Negro, the story goes, Drew in effect denounced the armed forces' policy of refusing Negro donors by telling his audience that there simply was no difference in the blood of human beings on the basis of race. Other versions of the story describe a much angrier Drew, one who stalked from the room when he was through saying what he had to say. No record of such a press conference has been found, however, for apparently it never was held. Still other stories have Drew—anxious for the position of director, not content with just that of assistant director—resigning because he was convinced that he would never, as a Negro, receive the promotion.

Over the years, after he had left the national blood program, Drew himself never commented upon his reasons for leaving. Or, as his old friend W. Montague Cobb put it: "Dr. Drew is not known to have murmured."[2] Really there was no need for him to comment because, among all the possible reasons for his leaving, rarely is the most obvious one (and the apparent one) mentioned: his leave of absence from Howard University was about to expire. It did expire at the end of April 1941, and his resignation came some weeks before the expiration.

An old friend of Drew's (though slightly younger than him), Dr. Burke Syphax (former chief of surgery at Freedmen's Hospital), in the summer of 1983 denied the rumors about Drew quitting over the race issue or any other issue. Said Dr. Syphax: "There had always been sort of an unspoken agreement that someday he'd return as chief of surgery. . . . He always planned on coming back home."[3]

Time and again Drew recorded in writing (and perhaps also spoke about) his desire to found a Negro "school of thought" in medicine at Howard and to gain both national and international recognition for the quality of medicine, especially surgery, taught at Howard and practiced at Freedmen's. He wanted to see a surgical resident training program at Howard that would turn out surgeons who were the equal of those trained anywhere, and he frankly saw himself as the instrument for making that dream come true.

Howard already had given Drew four months leave, and then had extended it another three months. The position of chief of surgery at Freedmen's Hospital was at stake, and if there was ever any doubt that surgery was Drew's main and abiding interest, it should be remembered that the very month in which his leave of absence expired, April 1941, was also the month in which he was certified, following a brilliant performance at Johns Hopkins on the examination given by the American Board of Surgery.

Actually, Drew returned to Howard a whole month before his leave of absence expired, on April 1 rather than April 30, while there is no evidence whatsoever that he left the blood program with any bitterness. On March 24 he wrote to Lenore how he hoped "to bring things to a sort of decent finish here before the end of the week." He continued: "There are some things that I will leave unfinished here which I naturally would like to finish, but I feel that the moment is propitious for pulling out and hence my decision to report for work at Howard a month before my leave is up."[4]

Drew always intended to return to Howard; he was expected to return to Howard; and his leave of absence from Howard was about to expire. Clearly, by April 1941 the national blood plasma program seemed likely to work, with or without Drew, though the production of dried plasma still had not been mastered. Together with numerous others, he had made it work. But it was not so clear that without him Howard could become what he envisioned for it. So he went home to Howard—and would stay there for the remainder of his short life.

NOTES

1. Clyde E. Buckingham, "Dr. Charles Richard Drew," (Paper for the American Red Cross, 1968), 28.

2. W. Montague Cobb, "Charles Richard Drew, M.D., 1904–1950," *Journal of the National Medical Association*, 42 (July, 1950): 243.

3. Interview with Dr. Burke Syphax.

4. Drew to Lenore, March 24, 1941, CRD Papers.

As stated in the notes to the preceding chapter, much of the material for this chapter, too, was taken from Buckingham, "Dr. Charles Richard Drew." Also used were: American Red Cross, *Dr. Charles Drew*, n.p.; Richard Hardwick, *Charles Richard Drew: Pioneer in Blood Research* (New York: Scribners, 1967), 132; Hamilton Bims, "Charles Drew's 'Other' Medical Revolution," *Ebony*, 30 (Feb., 1974): 92–93; *Report of Blood Transfusion Betterment Association Concerning the Project for Supplying Blood Plasma to England, Which Has Been Carried on Jointly with the American Red Cross from August 1940, to January 1941,* issued January 31, 1941.

1. Richard Thomas and Nora (Burrell) Drew, the parents of Charles Richard Drew (Moorland-Spingarn Research Center, Howard University).

2. Charles R. Drew at the age of approximately six months (Moorland-Spingarn Research Center).

3. Four of the five children of Richard and Nora Drew: (from the left) Joseph L., Nora, Charles R., and Elsie (Moorland-Spingarn Research Center).

4. Charles Drew (third row, fourth from left) at Camp Craft, August 1920 (Moorland-Spingarn Research Center).

5. Charles Drew (back row, extreme left) Dunbar High School basketball team, 1920–21 (Moorland-Spingarn Research Center).

6. Charles Drew (front row, fourth from left) Amherst College track team (Moorland-Spingarn Research Center).

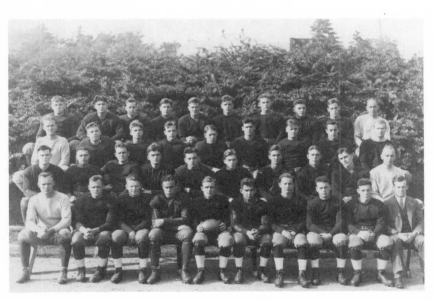

7. Charles Drew (front row, fourth from left) Amherst College football team (Moorland-Spingarn Research Center).

8. Coach Charles Drew (back row, extreme right) Morgan College basketball team, 1926–27 (Moorland-Spingarn Research Center).

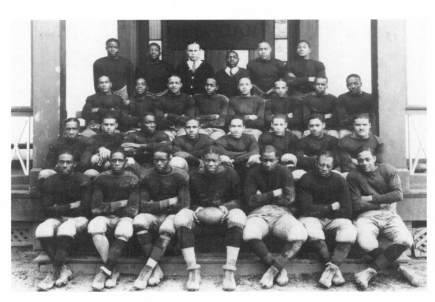

9. Coach Charles Drew (back row, third from left) Morgan College football team (Moorland-Spingarn Research Center).

10. Alpha Omega Alpha Medical Fraternity, McGill University, 1933. Drew (front row left) is seated next to Dean Charles Martin (photo furnished by Dr. Reginald A. Wilson, Vancouver, Canada).

11. Charles Drew with the Blood Bank staff (Moorland-Spingarn Research Center).

12. Charles Drew with the first mobile blood collection unit (Moorland-Spingarn Reserch Center).

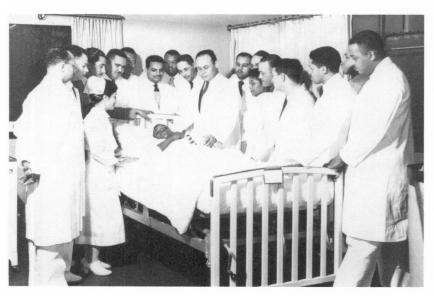

13. Charles Drew (center) shortly before his death, teaching at Freedmen's Hospital (Moorland-Spingarn Research Center).

14. Charles and Lenore Drew with their three daughters: (from left) "Bebe" Roberta, Charlene Rosella, and Rhea Sylvia (Moorland-Spingarn Research Center).

15. Charles and Lenore Drew with their four children: (standing, from left) Bebe, Charlene, and Charles, Jr., (sitting) Rhea Sylvia (Moorland-Spingarn Research Center).

16. The portrait of Charles Drew that hangs at the Clinical Center of the National Institute of Health (Moorland-Spingarn Research Center).

17. Charles Drew (standing) at a speaking engagement two days before his fatal accident (Moorland-Spingarn Research Center).

18. Site of Drew's fatal accident, near Haw River, N.C.—exact location just to right of telephone pole, where the small trees are (photo courtesy of Max M. Way, Alamance County Historic Properties Commission, 1984).

19. On April 5, 1986, at the dedication ceremonies for the marker located on the spot of the fatal accident: (left to right) Joseph L. Drew, brother of Charles R. Drew; Mrs. Charlene Drew Jarvis, Drew's daughter; and Mrs. Lenore Drew, Charles's widow. The bronze plaque on the marker honoring Drew reads as follows: "Charles Richard Drew, 1904–1950; black scientist and surgeon; pioneer in the preservation of blood plasma; medical director of the Blood-for-Britain project, 1940; director of the first American Red Cross blood bank, 1941; teacher to a generation of American doctors, Freedmen's Hospital, Howard University, Washington, D.C.; outstanding athlete, Amherst College and McGill University; member of Omega Psi Phi Fraternity; steadfast foe of racial injustice; died in Alamance General Hospital, 1 April 1950, after an automobile accident at this site. 'There must always be the continuing struggle to make the increasing knowledge of the world bear some fruit in increased understanding and in the production of human happiness'—Charles R. Drew" (photo courtesy of Max M. Way, Alamance County Historic Properties Commission).

20. Building that formerly housed the Alamance County General Hospital, Burlington, N.C., where Drew died (photo by author).

21. Two of the three physicians who worked to save the life of Charles Drew: (from left) Dr. Harold B. Kernodle and Dr. Charles E. Kernodle, Jr. (photo furnished by Dr. Charles E. Kernodle, Jr.).

9

Surgery: Drew's Chief Interest

When Drew took the oral portion of the examination for certification by the American Board of Surgery in April 1941, another legendary story was born. But apparently this one, unlike some of the others, is no myth, and it is proudly retold, even today, by physician friends who knew him. This incident took place, it was said, while a distinguished Johns Hopkins surgeon was questioning Drew about fluid balance in the human body, which of course was one of his earliest research interests and one that he had pursued when he first went to Presbyterian Hospital. The answer that followed was such a vast and learned discourse that the questioner sent for help from other surgeons who knew more about the subject than he (though not more than Drew). Just six months later, in October 1941, Drew himself was appointed as an examiner for the American Board of Surgery—the first black surgeon to receive such an appointment.

Promotions came at the same time—from assistant professor to professor of surgery at Howard, and from surgeon to chief surgeon at Freedmen's. A surgeon with smaller dreams might have felt that he "had arrived," but not Drew—he was but on his way. Along with his promotions, public recognition began to come, too. In April 1942, just six months after his appointment as an examiner for the American Board of Surgery, he received the E. S. Jones Award for Research in Medical Science from the John A. Andrew annual clinic in Tuskegee, Alabama. In June 1943 he was appointed a

member of the American-Soviet Committee on Science, in recognition of his interest in and knowledge of Soviet research in blood
preservation. In January 1944 he was appointed chief of staff at
Freedmen's Hospital, a post that he filled for two years, and the
following July he was awarded the Spingarn Medal by the NAACP
for his blood research and work on the plasma projects. A year
later, in August 1945, he was made chairman of the surgical section of the black National Medical Association. From 1946 to 1948
he served as medical director at Freedmen's Hospital. In 1946 he
was elected vice-president of the American-Soviet Medical Society
at its second annual meeting, while that same year he was made a
fellow of the U.S. chapter of the International College of Surgeons.
And in 1949 he was appointed surgical consultant to the surgeon
general of the United States. Yet despite all these achievements,
Drew was never—during his lifetime—allowed to be a member of
the American Medical Association. But why that is so is another,
longer story, treated in the next chapter.

    Indeed, Drew's career reflected his own sense of which area of
his life's achievements was most important. As he put it: "My chief
interest was and is surgery."[1] An outgoing, confident, ebullient
Charlie Drew wrote to an old McGill University classmate, Gladys
C. Hardwick, in 1944: "I feel that my life story as a physician has
just had its preface completed and the rest is yet to come."[2] Another old friend deftly recalled of him that "he was not wholly
indifferent to his value as a public hero."[3]

    Howard University Medical School and Freedmen's Hospital had
never known anything quite like Drew. There were others—the
surgeon Daniel Hale Williams in the late nineteenth century; Ernest Everett Just, the marine biologist; and, more recently, Drew's
contemporary, the anatomist W. Montague Cobb—who were, to
put it mildly, distinctly memorable men and fine scientists, but
Drew was in a class by himself, the awareness of which could not
have escaped him. For in addition to all his impressive professional
qualifications, achievements, and recognition, Drew possessed a
sense of geniality that was magnetic in effect—even when, at 2:00
in the morning, he walked into a surgical ward and greeted the
one or more tired residents and interns, together with the nurses
and orderlies on duty there. The effect—as those who were there
still remember—was magical.

Such a man, though, whether surgeon or engineer, made his colleagues and his peers look less distinguished, and the average and the mediocre appear even less so. Jealousy, if not enmity, followed, and though there is no clear record that Drew had enemies, he did have his share of critics and jealous colleagues. How could they help being at least envious of his well-known name, his high-placed contacts, and his ability to promote whatever it was he was interested in at the moment? Even the president of the university, Mordecai Johnson, who himself was no slouch at self-promotion, was annoyed, even angered, at how sometimes institutions or philanthropic agencies interested in advancing Drew's work at Howard contacted Drew directly rather than the president.

Drew also, not surprisingly, possessed a degree of myopia, say his critics, when it came to viewing the medical school as a whole, for he sometimes acted as if surgery were its only department. An easy talker, but intense in debate, he occasionally lost his sense of objectivity. Accordingly, there were those who found that Drew was not without his faults, which some felt were "many," and they violently disagreed with him and were angered by him.[4]

But surely Drew would have been less of a man and less of a surgeon had he not had some controversial traits and at times rubbed others the wrong way. Even mild Dean Adams had his critics, while President Johnson was viewed as both frightening and dangerous by the occasional faculty member whom he dared to lecture in the area of his own expertise, even if that discipline was in fact foreign to the president.

With Drew back at Howard to stay for the remainder of his life, a new phase in his life now began, as he became a trainer of surgeons. Research now took a back seat to teaching, though it continued along with publication. Drew had four papers appear in print, in which he was listed as either the sole or principal investigator, between May 1941 and 1951. Three of these papers related to his earlier blood work; the other was on the treatment of shock. Six more papers bore his name either as co-author or as a contributor; two were published posthumously.

Apologizing, as it were, for the little time available to him for research, in 1947 Drew wrote to President Charles W. Cole of Amherst College, his alma mater: "There is very little time for research, but the boys whom we are now helping to train, I believe, in time will constitute my greatest contribution to medicine."[5] After Drew's death, Dr. Paul B. Cornely, who succeeded him as medical director at Freedmen's, put the matter of Drew's priorities even more strongly. "He chose," he said, "to devote most of his energies and varied abilities to one all-consuming interest—the training of young Negro surgeons. He wanted to train Negro surgeons who would be able to meet the most rigid standards of specialization anywhere and place them in strategic positions throughout the nation so that they could, in turn, act as seeds for the growth of other centers."[6]

And toward that end, Drew was a taskmaster. Dr. Samuel Bullock, a lifelong friend and a distinguished surgeon himself at Freedmen's, remembered Drew as a "severe teacher." "That man," he said, "was a perfectionist from the first day I met him, and I'd known him since high school. He thrived on doing things—and having others do them—that he could take pride in."[7] Dr. Asa G. Yancey, one of Drew's most outstanding students, proudly remembered his old mentor as "warm, just, and understanding, but firm."[8] To Drew, Dr. Yancey recalled, standards were standards—they were the same for all. And no matter what one's background or race, those standards were not to be compromised, neither out of compassion nor in order to increase the number of black physicians. All the same, if Drew saw that one of his students was having trouble with some part of his residency, but believed that he was still capable of meeting his standards, he would undertake tutorial sessions for him—so long as he was convinced that the potential was there.

In the pursuit of his ideals Drew was personally spartan in the opinion of many. As a former athlete he neither smoked nor drank, and coming from a family where both the Bible and the church played a major role in daily life, he neither used profanity nor gambled. Dr. Jack White, retired chief of cancer research at Howard and another of Drew's stellar students, recalled how he jokingly said to Drew one day, in the presence of others, that he wondered why so few interns, residents, nurses, and others came to watch him, White, operate, while Drew always had a full house. Sternly, with no humor intended, Drew replied: "You'd have more people around watching you, too, if you would improve your manners."[9] Hurt, even angered by such a public rebuke, Dr. White said that he hurried after Drew and told him that he resented being talked to that way. After a moment, Drew apologized, but added that he *had* heard that White told off-color stories in the operating room, and he objected to that. Dr. White also recalled how Drew objected to the penny-ante gambling that sometimes went on in the hospital among interns and residents.

Another story concerned Drew's strong preference for neatness of dress and person among his students. A particularly unkempt medical student once was making hospital rounds with Drew, who remonstrated him for his appearance. The student pled "no time, too busy, too much work, etc.," to which Drew replied: "Well, *I'll* wash your clothes; *I'll* darn your socks; *I'll* clean your shoes. . . . !" Needless to say, according to Dr. Syphax, that student never appeared looking that way again.[10]

Drew also had a way of making a junior colleague whom he regarded highly look good. Once, said Dr. Syphax, Drew asked him to help him at the weekly conference where patients were presented in an auditorium setting, and the subject was amputations. The students all claimed that Drew did not need any "help"; he just wanted to make Syphax look good. Dr. Syphax remembered Drew as a "superb" teacher who not only taught, like any teaching surgeon, by letting students observe *how* he used a scalpel, for instance, but who also told them *why* he held it and used it the way he did, or why a clamp should be applied *this* way.

A part of Drew's training method, though, was for him to take special note of the ablest students, and when they had finished their residency in general surgery under him, to encourage them to go on for further training elsewhere in subspecialities such as gynecology, neurosurgery, cardiovascular surgery, and so on. Often it was Drew's connections that helped him place his former residents in such training.

In December 1948 the first residents trained by Drew went to Johns Hopkins to take their examinations for certification by the American Board of Surgery. His widow recalled how, anxiously waiting to hear the results, Drew went down into the cellar and commenced to tear apart an old coal bin, a task that he had been postponing. He was still worrying about how "his boys" were doing "up there at Hopkins competing with graduates of the top medical schools . . . with rich boys . . . boys who've had every advantage," when President Mordecai Johnson called to say that he'd just learned that the two top scorers on the examination had both been trained by Drew.[11]

Between 1941 and 1950, from the time that Drew returned to Howard until his death, Drew trained more than half of the black surgeons certified by the American Board of Surgery (eight of the total number); another fourteen, who were later certified, received at least part of their training from him. Dr. Charles D. Watts, later medical director of the North Carolina Mutual Insurance Company, and a Drew student, recalled his mentor this way: "He helped prepare a whole generation of surgeons, and a whole new thrust in training. And what he did at Howard didn't collapse when he died; it was continued very ably, by later Chief Surgeons: Dr. James R. Laurey, Dr. Clarence S. Greene, Dr. Burke Syphax, and Dr. Lasalle Leffall. Black surgical training has never been the same."[12]

A severe, demanding teacher, yet one who sometimes paid the travel expenses of some of his younger residents out of his own pocket so that they might attend medical meetings that he felt would benefit them, Drew was a regular mother hen when it came to keeping in touch with his former students. For instance, on October 31, 1946, he wrote to Dr. Jack White, the resident whom he had reprimanded for his "manners" in the operating room: "I know you must feel that I have sent you off to the far, cold northland [the U.S. Public Health Service at the Marine Hospital, at Brighton, Massachusetts] and left you to work out your destiny as best you could without further interest on our part. This is not true. We still love you and are extremely interested in what you do, what you think, and what you plan for the future." Then, on a professional and philosophical level, he continued:

> I took the liberty of reading to the fellows that section of your last letter which presented a comparative analysis of procedures there and those here. This type of information, I feel, is of inestimable value. Each service has a character of its own, and only when one knows how many services are run will he have sufficient background to select those routines from each which best suit his needs and skills. . . . Our horizons are being widened by the residents all the time and the things they write back, sharing with us, as it were, their daily experiences, enriches us all and at the same time forges the bonds which unite us even more firmly, so that each man is inspired to do more and more on his own in order to be worthy of

the fine companionship of such a group. In the individual accomplishments of each man lies the success or failure of the group as a whole. The success of the group as a whole is the basis for any tradition which we may create. In such tradition lies the sense of discipleship and the inspiration which serves as a guide for those who come after, so that each man's job is not just his job alone but a part of a greater job whose horizons we at present can only dimly imagine for they are beyond our view.

The thing which we have not had in the past is a group bound by similar training, aspirations and ideals to which we could feel that we belonged. The sense of belonging is of extraordinary importance to man as individuals and as groups. The sense of continuously being an outsider requires the greatest type of moral courage to overcome before actual accomplishments can be begun. Our fellows are rapidly creating something which gives them a sense of "belonging to." Within the protection of this feeling, they should be able to accomplish more than the fellows who have gone before.[13]

On a later occasion, Drew wrote of Dr. White that he was "an excellent student. . . . He is the seventeenth son of a rather poor Florida family, who has come as far as our Chief Residency almost entirely on his own in a rather strenuous competitive set-up. A year at Boston [at Brighton] as a Resident in Surgery at the Marine Hospital did much to give him poise and understanding in an environment in which, up until that time, had been a 'closed book' to him."[14] It is no wonder that Drew's students still speak of him in terms of admiration, and even reverence.

The same Charles R. Drew also found time the following year to write to a black Fort Worth, Texas, public schoolteacher who had written to him about how she had organized a program for her whole school in honor of Drew and his achievements:

There are so many things still unknown in almost every realm of knowledge, and the need for this knowledge is so great that in the vast majority of instances any new addition not only is accepted, but the individual who creates the work is accepted without very much regard to race, color, or creed. There are many difficulties to overcome, it is true, but our greatest difficulty still remains in the fact that we do not have very much that anyone wants. So much of our energy is spent in overcoming the constricting environment in which we live that little energy is left for creating new ideas or things. Whenever, however, one breaks out of this rather high-walled prison of the "Negro problem" by virtue of some worthwhile contribution, not only is he himself allowed more freedom, but part of the wall crumbles. And so it should be the aim of every student in science to knock down at least one or two bricks of that wall by virtue of his own accomplishment.[15]

Whether Mrs. J. F. Bates, the schoolteacher, read Drew's letter to her class or to the whole school, is unknown. But if she did, what effect, what impact, must those moving words have had upon at least one little black boy or one little black girl, sitting in a segregated Texas schoolroom in the year 1947?

Drew's "chief interest," as he once wrote, always may have been surgery, but his chief concern was life, and the full development of its potential, especially in those who, less free, had less reason to hope.

NOTES

1. Drew to Mrs. H. E. Harris, September 17, 1948, CRD Papers.

2. Drew to Gladys C. Hardwick, June 26, 1944, ibid.

3. W. Montague Cobb, "Charles Richard Drew, M.D., 1904–50," *Journal of the National Medical Association*, 42 (July, 1950): 245.

4. Paul B. Cornely, "Charles R. Drew (1904–1950): An Appreciation," *Phylon*, 11 (Second Quarter, 1950): 177.

5. Drew to Charles W. Cole, May 29, 1947, Amherst College Archives.

6. Cornely, "Charles R. Drew," 176.

7. Hamilton Bims, "Charles Drew's 'Other' Medical Revolution," *Ebony*, 30 (Feb., 1974): 88.

8. Interview with Dr. Asa G. Yancey.

9. Interview with Dr. Jack White.

10. Interview with Dr. Burke Syphax.

11. Lenore Drew, "Unforgettable Charlie Drew," *Readers' Digest* (Mar., 1978): 139.

12. Bims, "Charles Drew's 'Other' Medical Revolution," 96.

13. Drew to Dr. Jack White, October 31, 1946, copy given to the author by Dr. White.

14. Drew to Dr. Cornelius P. Rhoads, November 9, 1948, quoted in *A Century of Black Surgeons: The U.S.A. Experience*, ed. Claude H. Organ and Margaret M. Kosiba (Norman, Oklahoma: Transcript Press, 1987) vol. 1, 44.

15. Drew to Mrs. J. F. Bates, January 27, 1947, CRD Papers.

Hepburn, "The Life of Dr. Charles R. Drew," 23; Ben Richardson and William A. Fahey, *Great Black Americans,* 2d rev. ed. (New York: Crowell, 1976), 267; *Los Angeles Tribune,* January 7, 1947; Cobb, "Charles Richard Drew," 245; Cornely, "Charles R. Drew," 176–77.

10

Drew against the AMA

In western society, as early as the eleventh century, beginning with associations of merchants known as guilds, members of professions have sought to control the quality and price of their services. The merchant guilds also sought to control the quantity of goods offered for sale and to control guild membership so as to guarantee the members' social status as well. At about the same time, guilds of craftsmen or artisans also developed with much the same goals in mind—uniform standards of quality, regulation of the number of artisans, and, of course, protecting the social status of guild members. Implicitly, both the merchant and the craft guilds shared yet another goal (though it was not voiced as often as the others), namely, to regulate competition and thus guarantee a "fair return" to guild members—according to the guild members' interests, of course, not those of the general public.

Although guilds officially were abolished in England in 1835 as part of a general movement for social and political reform, some of the old ideas of the guilds reappeared, in both England and the United States, in the nineteenth-century craft union movement. Craft unions prevailed until mass industrial labor unions made up largely of unskilled workers arose in the twentieth century. In the United States industrial unions rose to power with the New Deal in the 1930s. Of course, the guilds are also mirrored in the associations of professionals, such as the American Bar Association

(ABA) and the American Medical Association (AMA), which arose roughly at the same time the craft unions did.

The gap between guilds, unions, and professional associations, such as the American Medical Association, may at first glance seem to be wide, but in fact it is not. The similarity between them is not always obvious to the public, of course, especially with an association that claims its chief raison d'etre is to guarantee the quality of medical care. The world of professional medicine, after all, cloaks itself with an aura of mystery, and the public is often too ready to believe that its doctors know best what is good for them. Often, perhaps even in general, they do, but that very concession points to the unseen power that knowledge gives to the world of medicine, especially organized medicine.

One way to see how small the gap is between craft unions and physicians, with their image as scientists and public servants, is to look at history. As a result of a schism that developed between physicians and surgeons in medieval England, until the eighteenth century, barbers and surgeons were both members of the same craft guild. Indeed, more often than not, the barber and the surgeon were one and the same individual.

Such is progress. At any rate, by the 1940s, Charles R. Drew, although an eminent black surgeon who also was an examiner for the American Board of Surgery, was not a member of the local District of Columbia chapter of the American Medical Association. And try as he might, he could not become a member—because of the racial restrictions of the local chapter (not the national body). In fact, Drew died without ever being accepted for membership in the AMA.

The reason for this was not pure and simple, naked and ugly racism at all levels of the AMA, though many black physicians see it that way. Sometimes, perhaps even in general, in many local chapters (where AMA membership is determined), racism *was* the prime motive for denial of membership to black physicians. This situation was more common in the South, though it was not restricted to the South. The national AMA organization, which had no racial restrictions, simply allowed itself to become "tarred with the same brush" of racism because of its exaggerated respect for the local rights of its chapters.

It might not be unfair to say, though, that certainly the majority of physicians, especially those who are inclined to be active in AMA politics (as officeholders and delegates to local, state, regional, and national meetings, for example) are usually political conservatives or ardent states' rights advocates when it comes to politics on the federal government level. But no matter which way one approaches the problem—as a physician who believes that the national organization of the AMA has no right to determine membership requirements for local chapters, or simply as a conservative citizen who believes that each state, not the federal government, should be allowed to determine who votes—when exclusion occurs, it means that the excluded then have no say at *any* level, whether in the context of the AMA or the United States political system itself.

The argument will not, of course, rest there, but it does seem fair to say that, as a national organization, the AMA—at least so far as membership requirements are concerned—for too long suffered from an exaggerated sense of states' rights, while at the same time it demonstrated a lack of concern for the rights of the individual physician, especially if he or she happened to be black.

Defenders of the status quo could, and sometimes did, resort to an extraordinarily simplistic defense of the AMA's hands-off policy toward the racial practices followed by *some* of the local societies. They pointed out that black physicians, after all, had "their own" national organization, the National Medical Association, which had existed since 1895. But this argument simply begged the issue. For instance, because of the power of the AMA (and its interest in respecting local standards), black physicians who were not AMA members could not enjoy hospital privileges (that is, they could not have their patients admitted to local hospitals and treat them there themselves). This policy drove seriously ill black patients to white physicians. It also sometimes forced black physicians to refer their patients to white physicians in order for them to be admitted to a hospital. Not surprisingly, this led black community members to lack confidence in black physicians because, like those in the white community, they did not know or did not realize that AMA membership was linked to hospital privileges. No wonder the black community often had the attitude: "Black doctors can't do anything for you except give you a few pills and hold your hand." Of course, in addition, denial of hospital privileges also meant that the black physician's continuing medical education would be hampered by the consequent lack of hospital experience. Furthermore, it was pointless in all but a tiny handful of instances to say, "Then let blacks establish their own hospitals." Cost took care of that, as almost wholly white communities learned when they tried to establish hospitals themselves.

Assuredly, too, black physicians were stymied in seeking research funds because they could not show that they had "met the standards" for AMA membership. And finally—though there were still other "penalties" for not having an AMA membership—there was the matter of pride and self-respect, not only in the black community, but in the larger medical world as well. How, for instance, did a physician as eminent as Charles R. Drew explain to a European or other foreign physician how it was that, though he was a certified member of the American Board of Surgery, he was not a member of the American Medical Association because his own local medical society in the District of Columbia did not accept black members? Indeed, not till 1952, two years after Drew's death, were black physicians accepted as members of his local AMA chapter.

The American Medical Association was founded in Philadelphia in 1847 for the purpose of raising the standards of both medical education and licensure in the United States. And it was needed, for the medical world of that day not only lacked more or less uniform standards for the training and licensure of conventional physicians, but it also included homeopaths and various eclectics. By the end of the century osteopathy, chiropractic, Christian Science, and various "cults" in electro- and hydrotherapy had also arisen.

In 1870 the AMA for the first time successfully used pressure from the national level to force a state organization to purge its ranks of homeopaths and eclectics. That year it called upon the Massachusetts Medical Society to get rid of both, which it did. Similarly, in 1882 the judicial council of the AMA barred the further representation of New York delegates until the state society disassociated itself from all homeopathic connections. Obviously, when it suited the AMA's national organization, it did not hesitate to tell the states what to do.

It was also in 1870 that the issue of racial exclusion from membership first came up during the annual national meeting, held in Washington, D.C. Dr. John L. Sullivan of Massachusetts offered this resolution: "That no distinction of race or color shall exclude from the Association persons claiming admission and duly accredited thereto."[1] Dr. Sullivan's resolution was sparked by the refusal of the committee on ethics to seat delegates from the medical department of Howard University because they were members of a local, mostly black, medical society known as the National Medical Society of the District of Columbia, which, said the ethics committee, admitted persons to membership who were not qualified physicians. If, said the committee report, Howard University had sent delegates who were not members of the National Medical Society, they would have been seated. However, that point is not entirely clear since, in any case, they were *not* members of the local chapter of the AMA, known as The Medical Society of the District of Columbia.

On the surface, to some persons at least, that action by the AMA committee on ethics at the national convention does not seem to have been wholly unreasonable. However, it is incredible that another sixty-nine years passed before, in 1939, the question of race in any form came before the national convention again. In the meantime, blacks did join the AMA whenever and wherever the *local* AMA society would admit them; and outside the South and the District of Columbia, admission was more or less commonplace.

In 1939 a resolution "urging that membership in the American Medical Association be not denied solely on the basis of race, color or creed" was defeated because such a resolution, if passed, would have implied that the county medical societies did not "have the right of selection of [their] own members, a fundamental principle in our organization."[2] Of course, in 1870, as we have seen, the *state* medical society of Massachusetts was pressured to get rid of its homeopathic and certain other members, and in 1882 the New York delegates were denied their seats because of the *state* society's connections with homeopathy. Apparently, telling a state organization whom it had to get rid of because they were *not* "professionally qualified" did not violate the AMA's "fundamental principle of organization," while telling a *county* society whom it had to admit because they *were* qualified did violate that principle.

To black physicians such an argument smacked of constitutional principle—but only when convenient.

Meanwhile, in 1895, black physicians and others—in Atlanta at the same Cotton States Exposition where Booker T. Washington gave his much-praised (by whites) "Atlanta Compromise" speech—had formed their own national organization, the National Medical Association (NMA). Prior to its second meeting—held in 1903 at Meharry Medical College, in Nashville, Tennessee—it was known as the National Association of Colored Physicians, Dentists, and Pharmacists. That year, its name was changed to the NMA, though for many years dentists and pharmacists were welcomed as members.

Meanwhile, in the AMA—but not until World War II—the question of restrictive membership policy based upon race that was practiced by many of the county medical societies began to come up with increasing frequency at the AMA's annual conventions, sometimes buried in committee, sometimes voted on by the House of Delegates, but always with the same result: it was a matter for the individual county societies to decide. In 1950, however, the House of Delegates adopted a resolution "urging" local medical societies with racially restrictive policies to take steps to eliminate them, but at the same time it reiterated the point that membership remained a local society responsibility. Interestingly, the resolution came from the delegates from Virginia. In 1952 the House of Delegates reaffirmed the stand of 1950: professional qualifications alone should determine membership, but membership was still a local responsibility. So, by the 1950s, the AMA was at the same point it had been in 1870.

Another eighteen years passed before the constitution of the AMA was amended, in 1968, so as not only to forbid racial discrimination in membership at *any level* in the AMA, but also to authorize the House of Delegates (only "in the event of repeated violations") to bar the seating of delegates from any state where such practices existed. Yet eighty-six years earlier, in 1882, the New York state society had been barred without further ado until it cleaned its house of homeopaths! Finally, during World War II, time caught up with the AMA and its restrictive racial policies—no matter what the excuse or at what level they occurred at—just as, on the larger American scene, time caught up with the "separate but equal" doctrine that had been enunciated in *Plessy v. Ferguson* in 1896.

Black membership, as we have seen, was first discussed at the AMA annual convention in 1870. Then the issue was not heard from again until 1939, popping up once more in 1944. Then, from 1948 to 1952 the issue was raised every year. Then in 1954, the year of *Brown v. The Board,* segregation on all fronts began to be challenged. The next year, in 1955, almost as if a silent "massive resistance" campaign had sprung up within the medical world, the issue of race was not mentioned, officially, at the annual convention; nor was it brought up from 1956 to 1960. It was back in 1961, ignored in 1962, but present every year thereafter except 1967, until it was laid to rest, finally, in 1968.

Understandably, a black physician and surgeon of Drew's stature would be bitter at what he considered the "hands-off" policy of the AMA on the question of racially based denial of membership to professionally qualified applicants. To Drew, and to other black physicians, it was a matter of simple logic that if the AMA could, at the national level, determine the professional standards one had to meet in order to join the local medical society—and then bar the seating of delegates from states that did not respect those standards, as was done in the case of New York in 1882—it could also force all qualified applicants to be admitted by using the same tactic.

In a bitter letter to the editor of the *Journal of the American Medical Association,* dated January 13, 1947, Drew began with the 1870 decision of the House of Delegates not to seat Howard University's delegation:

> I shall not argue the question for admission as it stood in 1870, but I do feel that this age-long policy of discrimination under whatever guise or pretext is one of the dark pages in the history of an organization which otherwise has many bright ones.
>
> The men in Washington, the nation's capital, are still rejected although there can be no doubt of their qualifications by any standards. . . .
>
> At Howard University for many years no physician has been considered for a position of professorial or associate professor rank in the preclinical area who has not earned a Ph.D. in his special field. In Freedmen's Hospital, the teaching hospital for the clinical years,

a man must have successfully passed his specialty board to be considered for the position of assistant professor. The chief of every
department and subdivision in the department is a certified specialist in name and practice. Match these standards with those of the
great hospitals of the land and they will be found good, but it [the
AMA] will not grant them the privilege of discussing common problems with fellow physicians in the learned councils of the American
Medical Association now celebrating its one hundredth birthday.
One hundred years of racial bigotry and fatuous pretense; one hundred years of gross disinterest in a large section of the American
people whose medical voice it purports to be—as regards the problem of Negroes which it raised in 1870; one hundred years with no
progress to report. A sorry record.

The American Specialty Boards accept a man on the basis of
merit; the American College of Surgeons has recently [1945] erased
the infamous policy of discrimination and has made a man's ethical
and surgical standards the sole measuring rod; the International
Colleges [Drew was a member of the International College of Sur-
geons] open their doors to men of like training and interests regardless of race or nationality; but not the great American Medical Association. If a small minority of county or state chapters persist in
wagging the whole body, and the body as a whole makes no move
to trust its own destiny, then it must be considered a body without
true strength and purpose, or one which likes the way it is going.
The American Medical Association should not start its second century with unfinished business of this kind making a mockery of its
continuous protestations of leadership in medicine under the great
and free American way of life.[3]

Shortly, Drew wrote again, having received a reply that only reiterated the old "membership in the AMA is a matter determined
by the local societies" argument: "You know and I know that it is
utterly impossible for a Negro physician to become a member of
a county medical society in the south. The American Medical Association has stood behind the by-laws which make this so as
though God himself had written the by-laws and that they were
immutable through the ages. These by-laws can and, I think,
should be changed." Negro physicians, he reminded editor Morris
Fishbein, "are a real and vital part of American medicine and
should no longer have to explain on every application blank why

they are not eligible for membership in the A.M.A." In a litany of anger and exasperation, he continued: "It is an unwarranted stigma. It is a cause of repeated humiliation. It is a constant indictment of the principles on which the American Medical Association is supposedly founded."[4]

Within a week, Drew had a reply, written by George F. Lull, secretary and general manager of the AMA: "The only way that this matter can be brought up in the House of Delegates is for a delegate to introduce it. . . . As you know, the American Medical Association cannot dictate any policies . . . as we are organized as a federacy of constituent organizations, so that even if a resolution was passed by the House of Delegates the state and local societies still could refuse to comply with it."[5] So there it was again. Nothing could be done, short of changing the by-laws of the AMA. But Secretary Lull did not mention that possible route.

Drew's experience with the American College of Surgeons was equally frustrating, for the same reasons. In 1945, the year in which the college accepted its first black member, Drew wrote to his old teacher and colleague, John Scudder:

> My first complaint against the College, of course, is, and has been, its bigotry; but probably a larger complaint would be that its admission requirements are too ill-defined and its standards too low for any institution which pretends to be representative of the best in American surgery. My contact with both the Canadians and the British has made it manifestly clear that they consider the American College of Surgeons to some degree a social organization whose scholastic and professional requirements, therefore, are purely secondary.[6]

Drew apparently had applied for membership in the college earlier that year, but for some reason, even though he was certified by the American Board of Surgery, he was denied membership. He believed that the reason was bigotry, as he wrote Scudder. In early 1950 Drew prepared to apply again, and he wrote to Dr. Robert J. Coffey, professor of surgery at Georgetown University College of Medicine, for permission to use his name as a reference. Coffey replied that he would be delighted to support him.

Death, however, intervened, and it was not until November 11,

1951, more than a year and a half after Drew was buried, that the American College of Surgeons issued him, posthumously, a certificate of fellowship.

NOTES

1. *Proceedings of the American Medical Association* (1870), 65.
2. Ibid., (1939), 82.
3. Drew to the editor of the *Journal of the American Medical Association,* January 13, 1947, CRD Papers.
4. Drew to Dr. Morris Fishbein, editor, *JAMA,* January 30, 1947, ibid.
5. George F. Lull to Drew, February 5, 1947, ibid.
6. Drew to John Scudder, September 10, 1945, ibid.

Proceedings of the American Medical Association for the years 1870 to 1968; John G. Burrow, *AMA: Voice of American Medicine* (Baltimore: Johns Hopkins University Press, 1963), 1–6; Drew to Dr. Robert J. Coffey, January 25, 1950, CRD Papers.

CHAPTER

11

"Dear Lenore" II

Drew's widow wrote of him nearly a quarter of a century after his death, how, even upon first meeting him, she was struck by his demeanor, which was as if he were from "another—a more old-fashioned and courtly—time and place."[1]

Drew was also old-fashioned in another way. He wrote long, informative, and revealing letters about what he had seen—he was an artist at description—and he wrote to Lenore the kind of love letters that not only told her what he thought of her, but revealed his innermost soul as well. And sometimes, apparently, his letters were just too much for her—"so philosophic that *anyone* could read them," she complained—when she obviously preferred something more intimate and traditional.[2]

For Drew, seemingly, his writing was a catharsis; it was to him, a nondrinker, what an evening drink or two is to many people. It caused him to relax, to unwind; and in unwinding he came to confront and to know himself better, like a lonely man in a bar with only the bartender to talk to. Confession came easily.

But not all his letters were "heavy," as we have seen. For instance, from New York, on Sunday, September 29, 1940, just after he had arrived back in the city to assume the post of medical supervisor for the Blood for Britain program, he wrote to Lenore:

> I sit now on the eleventh floor of the Y.M.C.A. and I thank my stars
> that this is only a transient abode, that I have a home of my own,
> that you are there and Bebe [his daughter and first-born, named

93

"Bebe" for Blood Bank, was born on August 8, 1940] is there, and it is cheerful, bright, happy, and comfortable. A single little room always seems to hem me in so tightly.

I'll be busy here but I have just been thinking how terribly busy you are there and after pay day, even more so. All the bills to pay, the curtains to fix, the covers to make, the studio couch frame to get built, another chair to find, scatter rugs to find, a baby carriage to get, new clothes to purchase, your abdominal muscles to tighten up by daily exercise, your food to get (enough of it) and the thousand other details of owning a house you wanted to be absolute boss of. Of course you will spend time missing me as I do you.[3]

In early December, after he had moved out of the "Y" and the blood program was going smoothly, Lenore came to New York and spent a weekend with him. He promptly wrote and told her how much he had enjoyed it. Then he wrote of attending, on the same day, "three meetings in a row—the first, down on Wall Street, the second, at the Commodore Hotel (swell lunch) and the third, at the American Red Cross. Quite a busy day." He continued:

It was decided to bring this work [the Blood for Britain program] to a close on the first of February. That is the answer as to when I shall be home for good. Before that time I shall have to write up the experiences of this association in this work in order that they may be available for other groups which might undertake such an adventure. It has been great fun. I have made contacts that I may have waited a lifetime to make in the ordinary scheme of things. One can not tell what the future of anything is going to be in times as turbulent as these, but up to now fate and chance have been very kind to me. I have gained insight into so many things that I did not clearly understand before I started this job.[4]

Just before Christmas, 1940, Drew took time out from the Blood for Britain program to take the written portion of his examination for certification by the American Board of Surgery (the oral portion did not come till April 1941). Upon receiving the results, he wrote: "Just got word that I passed the American Board of Surgery written examination. That is quite a Christmas present." Also, "To make your day very happy, we just received a cable from England stating that since the standardization of technique (that's when I took over here) no more infected material has arrived in England."[5]

In early January 1941, he wrote, teasingly yet proudly, "You will be pleased to hear that the State Department has considered your husband too valuable a citizen to expose himself to the rigors and dangers of the European scene at this time; therefore, they will not issue a passport." (A proposal had been made that a team of three physicians be sent to London to study the British blood program, but Red Cross headquarters had killed it.) He continued, "I do not know what the next step is at this time, but whatever it is I am pretty sure, I believe, that your hubby will be in the middle of it. The first chance that I get I will come down and discuss the future of this rapidly increasing little band of Drews."[6] (His second daughter, Charlene Rosella, was born on July 31, 1941.)

On February 4, 1941, the national blood collection program got underway, so that Drew was unable to come home "for good," as he had promised. This was a great disappointment for Lenore, so he wrote her a letter to ease her loneliness, and one that shows how much her husband was a philosopher-poet at heart.

> For you, I know, it has been a disappointing period. Our separation has caused us to miss much that we might have shared together. For this I am sorry. Many of the days and nights have been lonely here for me. I know that they have been much more lonely for you, but from times immemorial men who have beat out new paths into unknown regions have had to strike out alone, leaving all that was dear behind. These have been new paths that I have been treading, Lenore, as new as the uncharted seas that the early sailors defied, as strange as the new lands early explorers mapped while good wives waited in fear and loneliness lest the wandering ones fail to return. Yet, it has always been true that where one man dared to go, others would follow, and these, the ones who followed after, often brought their whole families along and knew more joy than those who first came that way, and some of those who came along later, were the children of those who had gone before and their joys were a recompense to those who had gone ahead, the lonely ones. Maybe Bebe will someday live and laugh and work under conditions which will make you glad that during long, apparently useless days you pushed back the tears and lived alone while I—I found new places in which to grow.[7]

Just six weeks later, though, on March 24, 1941, as Drew prepared to come home to Howard, for good, he was able to write:

Now we shall have a chance to see for the first time, really, just what
married life is like. Up till now we have been more like sweethearts
with special privileges, than man and wife. Do you think you can
take it? Having a man around the house in the way all the time. No
more sleeping in, meals to get on time, though the culprit may not
always show up, visitors to entertain, telephones ringing at weird
hours of the night, tales of my atrocities in the hospital to put up
with, etc. I think perhaps there may be a few things that I may add
to your happiness to make up these disrupting influences in your
life—for instance I can bring the baby carriage up the steps at night;
I can wax the floors (if I think it will not hurt my hands). I can take
you to movies (when I am not on call) and I can help you get
the back room straight. Perhaps I can put in some flowers in the
back yard. I think of you tonight and I am filled with longing to be
near you.[8]

Charlie and Lenore's marriage, however—like most, if not all,
marriages—was not without its strains. It was at times, perhaps,
complicated by Lenore's sense of dignity, of reserve, of coolness
even. The Drews were a close-knit family, but one in which daugh-
ters- and sons-in-law were embraced with equal warmness—but
this was not for Lenore. She would not stand for it. Perhaps her
temperament just would not allow her to do otherwise. She was
"Mrs. Drew," not just another "Drew daughter"; and she wanted
Charlie all to herself—a not wholly incomprehensible reaction,
though it may have seemed selfish to others.

Little things, too, as is so often the case, were the source of their
most noticeable differences and sometimes caused discord. For
instance, Charlie was exact in all that he did; he was a perfectionist. Lenore was less so, which led to disagreements over house-
keeping, over raising the children, even over casual dressing on her
part. It was not, however, a simple matter of *her* failings. Perfectionists always make those about them at least uncomfortable, and
worse, they have a way of expecting, and even demanding, that all
others be perfectionists, too.

Nevertheless, Lenore was not unaware of her possible failings, if
failings they were. For instance, when a family friend, the poet
Georgia Douglas Johnson, sent her a little literary homily titled
"The True Wife" and wrote at the bottom of it, "My friend: This
reminds me of you," Lenore wrote just below that, "I wish it did."

It went this way: "Where'er the true wife comes, the home is always round her. The stars alone may be over her head, the glowworm in the night, cold grass may be the only fire at her feet, but home is wherever she is and for a noble woman, it stretches far around her. Better than oiled cedar or painted with vermillion, it sheds its quiet light afar for those who else were homeless."[9]

On Charlie's part, he told Lenore bluntly on February 24, 1940, of his inability to "write eulogies about the powers of pure reason that my wife is gifted with," for "I may be a great flatterer but I am not a liar." And he continued in that vein. Yet that same letter ended with these words: "If I told you a thousand times, I couldn't love you any more than I do, and in the best way I know I'm trying to be worthy of your love."[10]

Lenore was always in his thoughts, and when he was away from home he regularly found time (throughout their marriage, and not just in its early months or years) to write, often in great detail, of what he had seen, what he had been doing, and, most of all, what he thought—about life, about the future, and always about his love for her.

In the summer of 1949, less than a year before his death, Drew was appointed as one of four physician consultants to the surgeon general of the United States and was sent to Europe to inspect American military medical facilities there and then recommend any needed improvements or changes. Although he was paid for his services, that trip was really the only genuine vacation Drew ever had. And he enjoyed it, but not so much that he forgot to share it with Lenore in regular letters. In fact, Drew would have made a great guide for the vicarious travelers of the nineteenth century, who depended upon the popular travelogue accounts of their day. (These were written by a few world travelers possessed of both some minor literary skills and the economic wherewithal to afford travel, yet not too proud to try to recover some of their expenses through the sale of their travelogues.)

From Munich, Germany, on July 6, 1949, Drew wrote Lenore about the still-visible destruction left by the war:

This is the queen city of Bavaria. On entering it, as in the other cities, there is a feeling of utter destruction. For blocks one can see nothing but empty walls and rubble, shells of magnificent buildings

standing stark against the sky with their empty windows like the
hollow eyes of skeletons looking out into nothingness. One cannot
truly describe it, only feel it.

One cannot enter town after town like this without being almost
overwhelmed. It seems almost impossible to rebuild all that has
been destroyed —either the buildings, their hearts, or their dreams,
yet these people are hard at it. Good night, sweet.[11]

A romantic, and a lover of both dance and music, Drew naturally
took to Vienna, Austria. "I do want to tell you about Vienna," he
wrote on July 10:

Vienna, while it has many buildings in ruins, was not devastated like
the German cities. It is still a great capital in spite of the fact that it
is the capital of a lost empire. . . . It is a city of lost dreams and music.
Every little cafe has music. I have not had a meal outside of the
hospital where there was not music—all kinds—from Beethoven to
very good American swing. The one defect in the picture is the fact
that we are always with colonels or generals who, of course, do not
indulge in the pleasures of the G.I.'s and who at all times are playing
a game of bluff with the Russians and conduct themselves in an
absolutely impeccable manner. We, as representatives of the Surgeon General, do likewise. Even this, however, has not spoiled the
enjoyment of the historical panoply stretched out on all sides. . . .

Quickly, though, Drew soon put all that aside and returned to
being the physician, writing: "I had the pleasure of making rounds
at the world famous *Allgemeines Krankenheit* (3,000 bed general
hospital). It is shabby and poor, treatment at least 15–20 years
behind ours, yet to watch Herr Geheimrat Professor Dr. Herman
Finsterer operate was a great privilege. He has done over 8,000
gastric resections. No one else in the world can even approach
this. . . ."[12] The next day, July 11, he wrote from Salzburg—romantically, again—"Outside my window tonight the river runs with a
sound that is both beautiful and lovely. I miss you tonight; I have
missed you all day. . . ." Then, after describing the peasants in the
fields, "cutting and sheathing wheat by hand as they have done for
centuries . . . a hundred pastoral scenes to delight the eye of an
artist," whom he had seen as he drove by auto from Linz to Salzburg, he described the city for Lenore:

Salzburg, like most of the other cities passed in the last week, lies
in a valley by a river with mountain peaks on all sides. It is an inter-

esting town in the daytime, unbelievably striking and beautiful at night when floodlights . . . on one of the mountain ranges light up the city. It looks like an Alpine scene on a great stage. It shines like a jewel in a great verdant crown of hills.

I miss you very much."[13]

Surely Lenore could be forgiven if she, at home with *four* children now, was envious and even a trifle jealous. (Their third child, Rhea Sylvia, had been born on February 15, 1944, while the fourth and last child, and the only boy, Charles Richard, Jr., had been born on October 30, 1945.)

The following Sunday, July 17, 1949, Drew anxiously wrote to Lenore from Nuremberg, Germany, "I have been away almost three weeks and I have not heard from you yet. . . . I should like so much to know how things are going at home. Tell me how you and the children are doing. If I don't hear from you I shall make a long distance call. I do miss you."

Nuremberg he found to be "a depressing place. Four years after the war most of the old city still is little more than a rubble heap." Then, perhaps because he was also lonesome for Lenore and the children and depressed over not hearing from her, he criticized, at length, the fraternization of American soldiers, including Negro soldiers, with German women and what it inevitably led to.

In this city there is a large detachment of Negro troops. Because I had no hospital duties I went out to the billets just outside of town and at the request of the chaplain spoke at morning services. This was my first contact with Negro troops on this trip. At chapel there were about 25 German brides, many of whom had their brownish offspring with them. This relationship there seemed quite alright; they looked like any other family group in church. Afterwards I had lunch at the officers' mess and picked up some rather interesting data. In the outfit I visited there are 900 men. During the last 19 months there were approximately 176 marriages. In January the authorities made the regulation stiffer and the rate has slowed up. Now marriages are not permitted until the man is within three months of his departure for the States. . . . What has simply happened is that the boys now live with girls out of wedlock. There have been 196 babies born to such couples during the last year. The chaplain estimates that 80–90 percent of the men have "homes" in the city. This, of course, infuriates many of the Germans but they dare not protest. The white soldiers do not like it and many fights ensue. Tonight, looking down on the main plaza of the city from my hotel room, I should say that at least 2/3rds of the troops were walking off arm and arm with some Fraulein within the first 50 yards from the bus stop. It is not very nice, as a matter of fact, makes one just a little sick in the stomach—but this is a victorious army, the Negroes are a part of it, there are few German men. The girls are still hungry and the Americans feed them, dress them, and fill their wombs. More than the towns have been destroyed—values are not the same.

Drew then reminded Lenore to "please save the things I send. They will make a nice addition to the kids' scrapbooks," and he bade her "Goodnight, my sweet." [14]

From Paris, on a rainy Tuesday morning two weeks later, he wrote that this is a "great city, full of grandeur and squalor, great beauty in the midst of much ugliness, a deeply religious place nestled in the most universal debauchery I have seen." Drew was no mere moralizer, however. He was interested, as a scientist and as a concerned human being, in *why* people behaved the way they did. He continued:

The moral code in Europe is a different thing from that at home and the attitude here in France requires a lot of understanding. In Germany, there is an extreme surplus of women and they are hungry. Moreover, they, throughout the war, were encouraged to have children; they still tacitly are encouraged to rebuild the nation's manpower. Many things are overlooked.

Here the naked female form is idolized, worshipped one might say, but woman's place is not a high one as a whole. There are so many of them, competition is so keen, and extra-marital relationships from kings to commoner such a part of France's history and present thing that a stranger has a difficult time establishing just where the values lie. Certainly it would be unwise to attempt it in a few days.

Like most tourists, Drew confessed that he had "gone about the business of crowding in as much of Paris as possible in a few days, largely through organized tours. . . . In this way one gets a bird's eye view of the overall picture. It is too much to take in in detail for it covers the history of Europe in all its aspects, but it does give a lot of material for future reading and thinking." Finally, he added, "Someday we must see this place together." [15]

A week later he was in London, but not for long—he only wrote one short letter from there. His first day he "got started early" and "had breakfast in the hotel—it was like all the food in London—has a great reputation for not being very good." But he "spent a marvelous day," and he ended his letter with this observation: "Here the people are slim, bright-eyed, clean-looking, the gentlemen impeccable, the women markedly different from Paris." Then, like so many Americans, he added, perhaps grudgingly: "One cannot but admire the British." [16]

A few days later he was back home at 328 College Street, on the campus of Howard University, his tour of western Europe completed—as was the vicarious tour made possible for Lenore through his letters.

NOTES

1. Lenore Drew, "Unforgettable Charlie Drew," *Reader's Digest* (Mar., 1978): 136.

2. Drew to Lenore, September 24, 1940, CRD Papers. All other letters listed in the notes for this chapter are also from the CRD Papers.

3. Drew to Lenore, September 29, 1940.

4. Drew to Lenore, December 9, 1940.

5. Drew to Lenore, n.d.

6. Drew to Lenore, January 9, 1941.

7. Drew to Lenore, February 10, 1941.

8. Drew to Lenore, March 24, 1941.

9. Georgia Douglas Johnson to Lenore, May 5, 1944.

10. Drew to Lenore, February 24, 1940.

11. Drew to Lenore, July 6, 1949.

12. Drew to Lenore, July 10, 1949.

13. Drew to Lenore, July 11, 1949.

14. Drew to Lenore, July 17, 1949.

15. Drew to Lenore, August 2, 1949.

16. Drew to Lenore, August 9, 1949.

Interview with Joseph L. and Grace Ridgeley Drew; Lenore Drew, "Unforgettable Charlie Drew," 136.

12

Of Myths and Men

Returning to that April Fools' Day, 1950, when the car he was driving overturned on a North Carolina highway, Charlie now lay near death. Ironically, he was injured in such a manner, with ruptured venae cavae (the two large veins that return blood to the right side of the heart), that blood transfusions of any kind were useless.

Since it was a Saturday, most of the mills in nearby Haw River and Burlington were closed, so there was not the usual stream of traffic at that hour (shortly before 8:00 A.M.) along North Carolina Route 49. But a small boy witnessed the accident, and there were passing motorists who had seen what happened. Someone summoned an ambulance from Burlington, and the highway patrol was notified. Both soon arrived, and the ambulance parked at the side of the road while the stretchers were brought into the field. Meanwhile, a motorist already had taken Dr. Ford to the hospital. Drew was placed on a stretcher and carried to the ambulance; Dr. Johnson, who was unhurt, was allowed to accompany him.

South on Route 49, to Haw River two miles away, the ambulance sped, then slowed down as it descended the gently curving road running through the tiny town, on down to and across the river for which the town was named. Climbing out of the little valley, the road soon straightened and entered Burlington, a bustling mill town whose biggest single employer was Burlington Mills, Inc.

Burlington (population 24,560, according to the census of 1950) lay approximately twenty-five and thirty-five miles, respec-

tively, west and northwest of the medical facilities associated with
both the University of North Carolina, located at Chapel Hill, and
Duke University, located at Durham, while twenty miles farther
west there were the hospitals of Greensboro. But there was no
time—and also no use, as soon it would be learned—to head for
any of those facilities. So it was to the Alamance General Hospital,
located on Rainey Street, approximately five miles from the scene
of the accident, that Drew was taken.

The Alamance General Hospital, originally known as Rainey
Hospital, was privately owned and operated by Dr. George Car-
rington and Dr. Ralph E. Brooks. Although the hospital was per-
manently closed the very next year and was replaced by the new
Memorial Hospital, it was regarded as wholly adequate for that day,
in terms of both staff and facilities, for a town the size of Burlington, especially since there were major medical facilities nearby in
Chapel Hill, Durham, and Greensboro. Also, both whole blood and
blood plasma were available for transfusions. Like virtually all hospitals in the South, it was racially segregated, but never was it a
"whites only" hospital, as later was said. The rooms for Negroes
were located on the basement level, just a few steps from the
emergency room. But there was only one emergency room, which
was used for patients of both races.

From the ambulance, with Dr. Johnson assisting, Drew was
rolled down the entrance ramp, located on the north side of the
building, and into the emergency room. While the attendants
sought to determine the extent of Drew's injuries, Dr. Johnson
recalled that "a tall, ruddy, brown-haired man in a long, white coat
[Dr. Harold B. Kernodle] came into the emergency room and ob-
served the patient. He asked in astonishment: "'Is that Dr. Drew?' I
answered, 'Yes, we had an accident on the highway.' In a commanding voice, he ordered emergency measures. At his request, fluids
were assembled and attempts were made to place a tourniquet
around the right arm."[1]

The attempt to save Drew's life involved not one, but three well-
trained physicians—the brothers Dr. Harold B. Kernodle and Dr.
Charles E. Kernodle, Jr., and Dr. Ralph E. Brooks, one of the two
owners of the hospital. Dr. Charles Kernodle recalled how he gave
Drew at least one blood transfusion before all three physicians
concluded that more blood would be useless and that nothing

more could be done beyond attempting to stabilize his condition. But as a last resort a phone call was made to specialists at the Duke University Medical Center, who, after hearing a description of Drew's injuries, agreed that nothing further could be done. Preliminary preparations for transferring him to Duke were then dropped.

Outside the emergency room, Dr. Johnson waited alone until Dr. Bullock, who had remained at the scene of the accident to gather up their baggage, was brought to the hospital by a highway patrolman. Bullock was then examined, and an x-ray taken of his back, and he was found to have suffered only superficial cuts on one hand. Dr. Ford's examination and x-ray revealed that he only had a broken left arm, but as a precaution he was admitted to the hospital for further observation and assigned to one of the basement rooms set aside for Negroes.

By this time, also present in the waiting room with Dr. Bullock and Dr. Johnson, was Dr. Charles Mason Quick, one of Drew's former residents, who had been summoned from his office at Winston-Salem. Almost two hours passed before one of the physicians attending Drew, Dr. Harold Kernodle, came into the waiting room. Dr. Johnson recalled that he told them all, "We tried. We did the best we could." [2]

On the death certificate, signed by Dr. Harold Kernodle, the time of death was noted as 10:10 A.M. Dr. Kernodle also noted that he had attended the patient from 8:30 A.M. till the time of his death, which, he wrote, was caused by brain injury, internal hemorrhage from the lungs, and multiple injuries to the extremities. Charlie Drew—"Big Red"—was dead, at the age of forty-five years.

Carrying Drew's personal effects together with all their luggage, Dr. Bullock and Dr. Johnson left the hospital in a taxi for the local railroad station and the sad return to Washington. Dr. Ford remained hospitalized. A hearse from the Sharpe Funeral Home of Burlington came for Drew's body, and that night it was sent by rail to the McGuire Funeral Home in Washington.

That afternoon the local paper, the Burlington *Daily Times-News,* reported in a prominent position at the top of page nine (a general news page, not a "Negro news" page, as sometimes is said): "Prominent Negro Surgeon is Killed When Car Wrecked Near Haw River." In the accompanying account the noun "Negro" always was capitalized, and the title "Doctor" was consistently placed before the names of Drew and his companions. The paper also noted that Drew was "recognized for his outstanding work in blood plasma during the war," and that he had had "several articles on blood transfusion and fluid balance published in medical journals and other publications." The headline, "Prominent Negro Surgeon . . ." stretched across three columns of the page, and the story consumed about four inches of each column. (Three days later, on Tuesday, April 4, the same newspaper noted that "Dr. John Ford, Negro physician from Washington, D.C.," had been released from the Alamance General Hospital.)

As well as the events of that day can be reconstructed more than thirty-five years later, and as clearly as they can be recalled by the surviving participants, the preceding portrayal of what happened to Charles R. Drew and his companions that April 1, 1950, is accurate. It is, after all, a credible story, and its veracity has been accepted by his widow as well as by many of Drew's former students, residents, and colleagues at Howard University and at the old Freedmen's Hospital. However, Drew's death is not portrayed this way in some of the history books that tell his story. The real story is not what most of the admiring public, both black and white, believes. They believe, instead—indeed, many *insist* upon believing, contrary to all the evidence and in spite of the eyewitness accounts—that Charles R. Drew "was allowed to bleed to death" outside of a "whites only" hospital that refused to admit him because he was a Negro!

Time magazine, for instance, in its March 29, 1968, issue, eighteen years after Drew's death, recalled how he "bled to death" after "he was turned away by an all-white hospital." And even *The New York Times,* as recently as June 14, 1981, said, in a philately column commemorating the issuance of a postage stamp in honor of Drew, that "the segregated hospital to which he was taken had no blood plasma that might have saved his life." The hospital had both plasma and whole blood, and at least one transfusion was given, but—with Drew's crushed chest and no way for the blood to get back to his heart because of his ruptured venae cavae—as Dr. Ford (who was there) has said: "All of the blood in the world could not have saved him." [3]

But the story lives on. A McGill University publication, the *McGill Reporter,* repeated it in its December 1981 issue. Fortunately, it brought a vigorous denial in a letter to the editor from Dr. Edward H. Bensley, professor emeritus of medicine at McGill, who had known Drew when he was an intern at Montreal General Hospital. Part of the evidence that Dr. Bensley had was a copy of a letter written by Dr. Ford, in which Ford tried to lay the "bled to death" canard to rest.

The late, popular television show "M*A*S*H" repeated the story in at least one of its episodes, while *Sepia*, a news and features magazine, somewhat in the style of *Life* but directed to a largely black audience, ran it in its December 1968 issue. In fact, even history books teach it. In 1967, William Loren Katz, in *Eyewitness: The Negro in American History,* a book designed primarily for high school students, passed the tale along to yet another generation. When the facts were called to Katz's attention, he corrected himself in a subsequent edition, published in 1974, but he left out any reference to his earlier mistake.

Where did the "allowed to bleed to death" story come from in the first place? And why will it not die in face of the facts? Why has it—apparently at least for some—even become such a cherished article of faith that it *cannot* be cast aside?

Among those to whom the origin of this rumor has been credited are both the black comedian and activist, Dick Gregory, and Whitney M. Young, Jr., the late executive director of the National Urban League. However, there is almost no likelihood that Gregory started it, because it has been around since Dick Gregory was a teenager. For instance, John Hope Franklin, one of the nation's leading historians, says that he has heard the story "almost since the day Charlie died."[4] Franklin was on the faculty of Howard University at the same time as Drew and knew him somewhat, and he was present at Drew's funeral. Also, Dr. Quick, the former student of Drew's who was at the Burlington hospital when his old teacher died, says that he first heard the rumor about five years after Drew's death, which would have been in 1955. If the rumor started almost immediately, as Dr. Franklin believes it did, it could scarcely have come from Gregory, who, in 1950, was an eighteen-year-old high school student in St. Louis. If it started somewhat later, it still preceded the incident in which Whitney Young, in October 1964, gave the rumor its greatest boost in circulation when he mentioned it in his nationally syndicated newspaper column.

In truth, *where* the rumor came from is really not that important, which is just as well since its origin probably never will be known. It well may have started in the black community of Burlington that April 1, 1950, as news of Drew's death spread across the nation. Or it may have started in the black community of his hometown of Washington, D.C. In the end, it is truly impossible to honestly speculate about the rumor's origin at all. Anyway, the entire nation, and not just the South, was no stranger to stories about how blacks had been turned away from hospitals for all sorts of facile *stated* reasons: no money, no room, "too serious for our limited facilities," and so on—when the *real* reason was race. Sadly, some of those stories were true, and perhaps because they were, they somehow became attached to Drew. He became a black martyr—the symbol for all those who actually were turned away because of their race.

Another possibility is that the rumor began with Bessie Smith's death in 1937. The legendary black blues singer was also supposed to have died outside a "whites only" hospital (in Memphis, Tennessee) that refused to admit her following an automobile accident. Chris Albertson, in a fine biography of Bessie Smith titled *Bessie* and published in 1972, sought to lay that myth to rest, but, as in Drew's case, "few were listening to the truth." Like Drew, Bessie Smith was involved in an early morning automobile accident, which occurred around 2:30 A.M., September 26, 1937, on a lonely stretch of road between Memphis, Tennessee, and Clarksdale, Mississippi. The first persons on the scene were two white men, one of whom was a young Memphis physician named Hugh Smith. There by the side of the road, Smith gave Bessie Smith what emergency treatment he could while his companion went to a nearby house to phone for an ambulance. The ambulance was somewhat slow in arriving, but when it did, its driver turned out to be black. He took Bessie to Clarksdale, where there were two hospitals—one for whites and one for blacks—only about a half-mile apart. The driver took Bessie to the black G. T. Thomas Hospital, where she was admitted. One of her arms had been severely injured and was amputated there, but within a few hours she died of shock and internal injuries. She was fifty years old, just five years older than Drew when he died.

Both were black, both were famous, both were injured in a car wreck in the South, and so on. It would have been easy to transfer the rumor from one to the other. Now both legends endure, haunting the memory of both Drew and Smith, who are too often remembered for the way in which they allegedly died rather than for what they did in life.

Drew was a perfect foil. He who had done so much to keep others from bleeding to death was himself the victim of that very fate, outside a "whites only" hospital that refused to admit him! It was a story easy enough for black America to believe in the 1950s, and even the 1960s. Now, in the 1980s, it seems necessary for some to believe it, perhaps because of the earlier *real* cases of blacks dying because they were not admitted to white hospitals. For instance, Golden Frinks, a former field organizer for the Southern Christian Leadership Conference, was quoted as saying that he will "raise hell" in order to see that the "true story" (in reality a myth) of Drew's death is not allowed to die![5]

Unfortunately, Mr. Frinks will be aided in his fight to perpetuate this myth by the fact that there never were any hospital records indicating what treatment Drew received at the Alamance General Hospital. Because Drew died in the emergency room, he was never formally admitted as a patient, so there never were any admission records. For each patient treated in the emergency room, only a card was made. In the confusion caused by a small hospital emergency room suddenly being presented with three physician patients at once—one of whom was the famed Charles R. Drew— apparently not even that card was completed. Perhaps, though, it was lost or discarded in the move to the new hospital building the next year.

Of course, one existing record of Drew's stay does remain—his death certificate—which indicates where and when Drew died, and from what injuries. Still, the loss, or lack, of Drew's medical record is unfortunate, as well as embarrassing, to both the hospital and the physicians who treated Drew. The record of Dr. Ford, on the other hand, who was admitted to the hospital, does exist at the new Memorial Hospital in Burlington, and it details his admission, treatment, and discharge.

Despite these problems, all three of the physicians who were with Drew when the accident occurred have done everything they possibly can to squelch the "allowed to bleed to death" rumor. (So has Dr. Quick, the former Drew resident who hurried to the side of his dying mentor.) For instance, Dr. Bullock, on April 4, 1950, just three days after the fatal accident, was quoted in the *Baltimore Afro-American* as saying that at the hospital they were treated with the "utmost respect and courtesy." Indeed, he said, the hospital staff and physicians "seemed shocked by the fact that it was Dr. Drew" they were treating. And concerning Dr. Bullock's reference to Dr. Charles Kernodle's phone call to the Duke Medical Center for consultation, the *Afro-American* even noted that Duke was one of the nation's leading medical centers.

Twenty-one years later, in 1971, Dr. Ford would recall the accident in vivid detail and write, "I remember the incident quite well." He continued as follows:

> Doctor Drew's cause of death was that of a broken neck and complete blockage of the blood flow back to his heart. Immediately following the accident in which he was half thrown out of the car, and actually crushed to death by the car as it turned over the second time, the doctors who were able to, got out of the car quickly and came to Doctor Drew's rescue, but it was of no avail because even at that time, it was quite obvious that his chances of surviving were nil. I was thrown 40 feet through the air and landed upright in a sitting position, after landing on my shoulder in a plowed field. When we went to the General Hospital in Burlington, North Carolina, we were given the utmost respect and courtesy. True enough, after I was admitted to the hospital, it was in a basement room, and unfortunately not in one of the regular rooms, however, they apologized profusely to me each day that I remained. They stopped their work immediately on white patients, clearing them out of the minor operating room, as well as surgery, and gave us instant and immediate care. We could not have been treated better.
>
> The statement about his bleeding to death because of refusal of treatment is utterly false. . . . I have issued this type of statement all over the country, but "nobody" wants to believe the truth about the matter.[6]

Dr. Ford was right: "nobody" wanted to believe the truth. So, eleven years after Ford's writing, in 1982 (thirty-two years after the fatal accident), Dr. Johnson, at the request of Mr. Joseph L. Drew (the brother of Charles R. Drew), wrote yet another disavowal of the "allowed to bleed to death" legend, for it was no longer just a rumor. In great detail Dr. Johnson described the entire incident, including the accident, the ride to the hospital, the treatment they all received there, and how one of the physicians told him of Dr. Drew's death. Finally, very carefully, with restraint and detachment, Dr. Johnson wrote:

> The treatment at the hospital, routine for accidental injuries in that region and specific for that period of time, suggests that a conscientious effort was made to revive Dr. Drew. It may be argued that given the same circumstances and the same period of time in other major medical centers, other results might have been obtained. But this would be pure speculation. Thus, we must assume that during the two or three hours that Dr. Drew lived, routine emergency treatment specific for that locality was administered and in spite of it, he failed to survive. There was no evidence to suggest that Dr. Drew received less than acceptable emergency treatment. It is hoped that this explanation of the management of Dr. Drew's injuries in the Alamance County General Hospital of Burlington, North Carolina, in the mid-morning of April 1, 1950, will put to rest the myths, innuendos, and rumors that suggest otherwise.
>
> As the least injured of the group, the one who accompanied Dr. Drew from the scene of the accident to the hospital in the ambulance, and the one who last saw him alive, I offer the above documentary of the event as I perceived it, to be a truthful, sincere, and factual account. It is a picture that has remained with me for over thirty years; one that I have tried to relate on many occasions, in many places, and when I have been questioned about the accident.

But, in closing, Dr. Johnson wrote, warmly and with deep feeling: "The loss was particularly acute for me professionally, for I was the last to be recruited by Dr. Drew, having been picked from the infantile paralysis unit of the John Andrew Hospital, in 1949, to become senior resident of the orthopedic service at Freedmen's Hospital and a member of his select circle of trainees.[7]

cally and humanly possible had been done for her beloved Charlie, and shortly after his death she wrote to Dr. Ralph Brooks, who, with the Kernodle brothers, had attended him at the hospital: "Please accept our many thanks for the efforts expended by you and your staff in an attempt to save the life of Dr. Charles R. Drew. Though all your efforts were futile, there is much comfort derived in knowing that everything was done in his fight for life."[8] In another context, she also wrote twenty-eight years after his death: "Near Burlington, N.C., he napped at the wheel for a moment. The car went off the road and turned over, and Charlie was crushed. Rushed to a neighboring hospital, he was too gravely hurt to be saved."[9]

But the legend lives on, as Dr. Quick even discovered at a Christmas party in 1981 in the home of Dr. Bullock in Washington, D.C. During the party someone remarked to Drew's daughter Charlene (Mrs. Ernest Jarvis, Oberlin-educated and a prominent political figure in Washington) how terrible it was that her father had bled to death because a "whites only" hospital had refused to admit him. Dr. Quick said that he and Dr. Bullock "stood up right away and said the story was a lie. We knew. We were there."[10]

Back home in Fayetteville, North Carolina, where he had moved from Winston-Salem, Dr. Quick demonstrated to a news reporter how universal, pervasive, and enduring the legend was. He summoned into his office a young black physician who had just completed medical school and asked him, "How did Dr. Charles R. Drew die?" The young man quickly, without hesitation answered, "He bled to death after a whites only hospital in Burlington refused to admit him."[11]

NOTES

1. Walter R. Johnson, "April 1, 1950," November 15, 1982, Archives, Headquarters, American Red Cross, Washington, D.C.

2. Ibid.

3. John R. Ford to Devra M. Breslow, March 12, 1971, copy in possession of the author.

4. *Greensboro* (N.C.) *Daily News and Record*, July 11, 1982.

5. *Greensboro Daily News*, July 14, 1982.

6. Ford to Devra M. Breslow.

7. Johnson, "April 1, 1950."

8. *Greensboro Daily News and Record,* July 11, 1982.

9. Lenore Drew, "Unforgettable Charlie Drew," *Readers' Digest* (Mar., 1978): 140.

10. *Greensboro Daily News and Record,* July 11, 1982.

11. Ibid.

Amherst Afro-American Society, *The Black Student at Amherst* (n.d.), 14; *Burlington Times-News,* April 1, 1980; *McGill Reporter,* 14 (Feb. 3, 1982); copy of Drew's death certificate, CRD Papers.

13

Remembering "Big Red"

Back in Washington the afternoon of April 1, 1950, as word of Drew's death spread through Freedmen's Hospital, "it created . . . an explosion of grief . . . the like of which we have never seen. Medical students, residents, young attending staff members, colleagues, and employees at all levels and in all categories wept unabashedly and unashamedly." [1]

Drew's family decided that the funeral would not be held till 1:00 P.M., the following Wednesday, April 5. In the meantime, from Tuesday noon till 10:30 that night, and on Wednesday morning from 8:30 till 11:00, the body lay in state in the Andrew Rankin Chapel, just inside the main gate to Howard University. The funeral service, with the Reverend Jerry Moore officiating, was held in the Nineteenth Street Baptist Church, which Drew had attended as a child and as an adult. The church was full, and a delegation from New York, including both Dr. Allen Whipple and Dr. John Scudder, was present. In a moving eulogy Dr. Mordecai Johnson said, "Here we have what rarely happens in history . . . a life which crowds into a handful of years significance so great men will never be able to forget it." [2]

Drew's body was borne from the church by Judge William H. Hastie and Howard University colleagues, Professors Clarence Greene, Mercer Cook, Burke Syphax, W. Montague Cobb, Leonard Hall, and R. Frank Jones, then taken to the Lincoln Cemetery in Suitland, Maryland, just two blocks from the District of Columbia line. Earlier generations of Drews had been buried in the old and crowded Harmony Cemetery, located at Eighth and Rhode Island Avenue, NE, but all the graves there, in a few years, would be moved to the new Lincoln Cemetery where Charlie—"Big Red"—was now laid to rest.

The day after the funeral, the *Washington Post* on its main editorial page called Drew one of the "most gifted of American surgeons," one who "chose to devote his gifts to the advancement of medicine rather than to the advancement of personal career or to winning the monetary rewards that were easily within reach. . . . He will be missed, however, not alone by his own race but by his whole profession and by men everywhere who value scientific devotion and integrity."[3]

Letters of condolence streamed into the Drew home from, among others, D. O. ("Tuss") McLaughry, his old coach at Amherst; Pearl Buck, author of *The Good Earth;* John Hope Franklin, the historian; Dr. Dewitt Stetten, president of the Blood Transfusion Betterment Association; Dr. R. W. Bliss, major general and surgeon general of the United States; Mary McLeod Bethune, founder of famed Bethune-Cookman College and former president of the National Council of Negro Women; and Dr. Arnold S. Jackson, secretary of the United States chapter of the International College of Surgeons, of which Drew was a member.

Coach McLaughry wired: "Charlie's untimely passing is a loss not only to his many friends, but to all humanity. He was one of the finest individuals I have ever known. My close friendship with him at Amherst and afterward is something that I will always cherish."[4] And in Massachusetts, at Amherst, Drew was remembered as "a great football player, a great alumnus of Amherst, a great doctor, and a great American."[5]

In addition to his widow, Lenore, Drew was survived by his four children: "Bebe" Roberta, aged nine; Charlene Rosella, eight; Rhea Sylvia, six; and Charles Richard, Jr., four, all of them scarcely old enough to remember little more about him other than that he was their father. Drew was also survived by his mother, Nora, aged seventy; a brother, Joseph L.; and two sisters, Mrs. Nora Gregory and Mrs. Eva Pennington.

Living always upon a modest salary rather than pursuing the

lucrative private practice he might have had (if he had cared more about material things and less about doing good), Drew was generous to a fault ("Giving people the shirt off his back was his favorite pastime," according to his widow).[6] It is no wonder then, that the estate that Drew was able to leave to his wife and children was modest. At the time of his death, Drew was earning only about $7,000 a year at Howard, while any income from private patients (of which 25 percent went to Howard) and miscellaneous income probably did not bring the total to more than $10,000. For instance, according to Drew's surviving income tax records, for 1943, Drew reported a gross income of $5,548; for 1945, $7,303; and for 1947, $8,199. Reportedly, he had offers as high as $20,000 from pharmaceutical companies to head up research projects.

For some years, however, Drew had contributed to an endowment plan; reportedly more than half of his salary went to it. He was able to set aside so much of his income not only because of his modest tastes, but because the house in which he and his family lived belonged to Howard University. The endowment, together with three-fourths of Drew's salary—to which Lenore was entitled as the widow of a Howard University faculty member killed while performing a university function—enabled her to remain at home with her children till 1966, when the youngest was twenty-one. The family's home moved, however, from the university-owned house at 328 College Street to 4409 Eighteenth Street, NW. The move and the new house were paid for with funds raised from the public through the Charles R. Drew Memorial Foundation (founded almost immediately after his death). Lenore and the children moved into the new home in February 1952, with the announcement that on April 1, the second anniversary of Drew's death, she planned to hold an open house for the contributors.

Always—and still today—friends, colleagues, and family remember Charlie as they knew him. His widow, Lenore, remembers him as a "simple and uncomplicated person," who did not "care much for complicated people."[7] Perhaps this trait helps explain his fondness for western movies, where the good triumphed over the bad. Others may not have seen him as quite so "simple and uncomplicated," unless they saw him at home, for Drew's home was his castle—it was where he unwound. And on at least one occasion,

Drew made it clear to Lenore that at home he was not looking for either intellectual discourse or "an argument on a purely masculine basis."[8]

According to Lenore, Drew was always a "natural man, without pomp."[9] He was enthusiastic about everything he did, including gardening, cooking, and playing the piano. He also slept heavily—perhaps because there was so little time for sleep.

Dr. Burke Syphax remembered Drew as a "gentle sort of man who would go out of his way to avoid offending anyone." In his bedside manner "he'd talk to the poorest, most ragged of our patients like he was talking to his mother. Believe me, in those days, that was not at all common."[10] That same politeness and graciousness also led Drew to send gifts to those who had done some small kindness for him. For instance, Dr. Asa. G. Yancey recalled how, when Drew was visiting the John A. Andrew Memorial Hospital in Tuskegee, he and his wife would have him for dinner. Drew always brought them a gift or soon sent them one.

Always a gentleman, and indeed something of a charmer, Drew also was a skilled politician when it came to getting what he wanted—and what he believed Howard University and the Freedmen's Hospital deserved. For instance, Dr. Syphax recalled the first time Drew, as medical director of Freedmen's, testified before a congressional committee on the Howard University budget. Before he gave his testimony, Drew "researched" the members of the committee, several of whom were southerners. He was thus able to tell those members just how many black students from each of their states were being educated at Howard—at no direct expense to their home states. That was shrewd politics.

For Drew, life was work; it was service. Aside from his family life, he had little social life. As for vacations, he never took them. When it came to extracurricular service, though, Drew was chairman of the surgical section of the National Medical Association; he was a member of the board of trustees of both the District of Columbia branch of the National Polio Foundation and the National Society for Crippled Children; he was a member of the board of directors of the District of Columbia chapter of the American Cancer Society; and he was active in the local YMCA.

Honors and recognition came remarkably early in life for Drew. Now, in death, friends and colleagues were equally quick to do more than just remember him. There was, first, the memorial fund that provided a home for Lenore and the children, and then, soon after, a Drew Memorial Scholarship Fund, which was established at Amherst. In just two years more than $10,000 accumulated in the scholarship fund, and in 1952 the first Drew Scholarship was awarded—to a pre-med junior who, like Drew, had a letter in football.

Drew has also received other posthumous honors. Public schools all over the country—north, south, east, and west—have been named for him, while in New York City—where Drew earned his Doctor of Science in Medicine degree and where all his blood plasma work was done—there is a public park named for him. In the Watts area of the city of Los Angeles there is the Charles R. Drew Postgraduate Medical School, which is affiliated with the University of Southern California and the University of California at Los Angeles schools of medicine. There is also a Drew postage stamp, in the denomination of thirty-five cents, that was issued in 1981 on his birthday, June 3. It was the fourth stamp issued in the Great Americans Series.

In Bethesda, Maryland, at the Clinical Center of the National Institute of Health, on October 13, 1976, a portrait of Drew was unveiled. The crowd in attendance filled the center's auditorium as well as an upstairs room where the ceremonies were shown on closed-circuit television. Drew's portrait then became the first one of a black man to hang among the center's gallery of Nobel Prize winners and former directors of the institute (see jacket cover and also Figure 16). It was painted from a photograph by Alfred C. Laoang, and it shows Drew in his white laboratory coat with the sun filtering through Venetian blinds onto a microscope and a slide fittingly containing a blood sample.

The next year, 1977, on June 15 in his hometown of Washington, D.C., some two hundred people, including thirteen members of Drew's family as well as civic and political leaders, gathered to dedicate the Charles R. Drew Blood Center, which occupies the main floor of the Red Cross Building at 2025 E Street, NW. At the ceremonies another portrait of Drew, painted by Betsy Graves Reyneau (also from a photograph), was unveiled. It hangs at the main entrance to the blood center bearing his name.

Most recently, on April 5, 1986, a six-foot granite marker bearing a bronze plaque was placed at the spot near Haw River, North Carolina, where the fatal accident took place (see Figure 19). Nearly four hundred people, including members of Drew's family, were present when his daughter Charlene unveiled the marker, which was financed through private donations. At the ceremonies, Dr. Charles Watts, one of Drew's former surgical residents, said, "The marker will say to all men that a great man lost his life here."[11]

So many accomplishments, and so much deserved recognition, for a man who died shortly before his forty-sixth birthday. What else might he have accomplished had he but lived out a normal life span? None can say, for none can know. But what he did accomplish was enough, and more, to assure that "Big Red" long would be remembered—as athlete, as scientist, as surgeon, and as teacher.

NOTES

1. Paul B. Cornely, "Charles R. Drew (1904–1950): An Appreciation," *Phylon*, 11 (Second Quarter, 1950): 176.

2. *New York Times,* April 6, 1950.

3. *Washington Post,* April 6, 1950.

4. Hepburn, "The Life of Charles R. Drew," *Our World* (July, 1950): 29.

5. *Amherst Journal,* April 7, 1950.

6. Undated clipping, Amherst College Archives.

7. *Miami Herald,* April 9, 1969.

8. Drew to Lenore, February 24, 1940, CRD Papers.

9. *Washington Post*, October 14, 1976.

10. Hamilton Bims, "Charles Drew's 'Other' Medical Revolution," *Ebony*, 30 (Feb., 1974): 93.

11. *Virginian-Pilot*, April 7, 1986.

Hepburn, "The Life of Charles R. Drew," 29; Drew's personal income tax records, CRD Papers; *Washington Post*, February 14, 1952; *New York Times,* April 3, 1950; interview with Dr. Asa G. Yancey; W. Montague Cobb, "Charles Richard Drew, M.D., 1904–1950," *Journal of the National Medical Association*, 42 (July, 1950): 244–45; *Amherst Journal,* April 7, 1950; *Amherst Alumni News,* 5 (Oct., 1952), 50; *Washington Post,* June 16, 1977; *New York Times,* June 14, 1981.

Bibliography

This study, or biographical interpretation, could not have been written without access to the Charles Richard Drew Papers, located in the Moorland-Spingarn Research Center, Founders Library, Howard University, Washington, D.C. As collections go, it is not an especially large one, and, unfortunately, virtually all of the correspondence is for the years 1939 to 1950—but it is a rich one. By far, the most valuable letters are those that Drew wrote to his wife, Lenore, from the time he first met her until just before his death. The papers also include the usual memorabilia, consisting of programs, posters, clippings, invitations, financial papers, tributes, and so on. Not so usual are the collection's eyeglasses, laboratory coats, football jerseys, graduation robe (with cap and three hoods) medical instruments, and prescription pad. Of this last group there was little that this biographer could "use" in a literal sense, but he was certainly made the richer for having seen and handled those objects. Finally, there is a superb collection of photographs, covering virtually Drew's entire life. Nearly all of the photographs that appear in this book came from the Drew Papers.

Almost (if not indeed quite) as valuable as the collection of personal papers in the possession of the author, were the recollections of Drew's family members, his medical colleagues (some of whom were childhood friends), and his former students (that is, surgical residents).

First among these many equals are Mr. Joseph L. Drew, the brother of Charles, and his wife, Grace Ridgeley Drew, and Mrs. Nora Gregory, one of Charles's two surviving sisters. Among former colleagues and lifelong friends, there are Dr. Samuel L. Bullock and Dr. Burke K. Syphax, both now semi-retired but, in fact, still quite active in medicine. Two of Drew's stellar students who were invaluable in helping the author get to know him were Dr. Jack White, retired chief of cancer research at Howard University, and Dr. Asa G. Yancey, medical director of Grady Hospital in Atlanta and associate dean, emeritus, of the Emory University School of Medicine.

Literature about Drew is plentiful, but much of it is of very limited value, since it either merely recounts all the myths about him or is itself based upon other published literature, which means that it tends to be repetitive. Among the best of this literature, though, is W. Montague Cobb, "Charles Richard Drew, M.D., 1904–1950," *Journal of the National Medical Association,* 42 (July, 1950): 238–246. Dr. Cobb grew up in Washington with Drew, they attended Amherst College together, and it was Cobb who encouraged Drew to return to Howard University after he completed medical school and his Montreal residency. Another very useful article that appeared shortly after Drew's death is David Hepburn, "The Life of Dr. Charles R. Drew," *Our World* (July, 1950): 23–29. Very useful also is Hamilton Bims, "Charles Drew's 'Other' Medical Revolution," *Ebony,* 30 (Feb., 1974): 88–96, which stresses Drew's role as a teacher or trainer of other surgeons—a role that Drew placed ahead of his blood work in importance. This work is also especially valuable because it makes great use of interviews with Drew's colleagues and former students.

The following articles are also useful: D. O. ("Tuss") McLaughry, "The Best Player I Ever Coached," *Saturday Evening Post,* 225 (Dec. 6, 1952), 184; Paul B. Cornely, "Charles R. Drew (1904–1950): An Appreciation," *Phylon,* 11 (Second Quarter, 1950), 176–77; Lenore Robbins Drew, "Unforgettable Charlie Drew," *Reader's Digest* (Mar., 1978): 135–40; Newton F. McKeon ('26), "Charles Richard Drew, 26," *Amherst Alumni News* (May, 1950); "Dr. Charles R. Drew," *The McGill News,* 31 (Summer, 1950), 56; Anne S. Bittker, "Charles Richard Drew, M.D.," *Negro History Bulletin,* 36 (Nov., 1973): 144–50; and the American Red Cross, *Dr. Charles Drew, Medical Pioneer* (pamphlet dated Nov., 1970).

Of much less value are two biographies and one joint biography: Richard Hardwick, *Charles Richard Drew: Pioneer in Blood Research* (New York: Scribner's, 1967); Robert Lichello, *Pioneer in Blood Plasma: Dr. Charles Richard Drew* (New York: 1968); and Emma Gelders Sterne, *Blood Brothers: Four Men of Science* [William Harvey, Marcello Malpigi, Karl Landsteiner, and Charles Richard Drew] (New York: Knopf, 1959). All three are juvenile fictional biographies, while the first two, by Hardwick and Lichello, are products of the sixties and the rush to give substance to black pride. Both are replete with dialog and the "thoughts" of Charlie Drew; in fact, the Lichello volume consists largely of dialog. For their purpose, and for the audience to which they are directed, they are perhaps justified and even useful, but those who want to know the real Charlie Drew should ignore them.

Useful in dealing with the background for Drew's work in blood and blood plasma research are: Elmer DeGowin, Robert C. Hardin, and John B. Alsever, *Blood Transfusion* (Philadelphia: 1949); Douglas W. Huestis, Joseph R. Bove, and Shirley Busch, *Practical Blood Transfusion,* 2d ed. (Boston: W. B. Saunders, Co., 1976); Albert R. Lamb, *The Presbyterian Hospital and the Columbia-Presbyterian Medical Center, 1868–1943: A History of a Great Medical Adventure* (New York: Columbia University Press, 1955); and of course, Drew's own "The Role of Soviet Investigators in the Development of the Blood Bank," *American Review of Soviet Medicine,* 1 (Apr., 1944): 360–69.

On the history of Howard University, see Rayford W. Logan, *Howard University: The First Hundred Years, 1867–1967* (New York: New York University Press, 1969). For the story of Freedmen's Hospital, see Thomas Holt, Casandra Smith-Parker, and Rosalyn Terborg-Penn, *A Special Mission: The Story of Freedmen's Hospital, 1862–1962* (Washington, D.C.: Academic Affairs Division, Howard University, 1975), which should be supplemented with W. Montague Cobb, "Numa P. G. Adams, M.D., 1885–1940," *Journal of the National Medical Association,* 43 (Jan., 1951): 43–52, and R. Frank Jones, "The Surgical Resident Training Program at Freedmen's Hospital," *Journal of the National Medical Association,* 52 (May, 1960): 187–93.

On the question of admission of Negro physicians to membership in the American Medical Association, see the *Proceedings of the American Medical Association* for the years 1870, and 1939 to 1968.

Newspapers that were helpful—the dates used are included in the notes at the end of each chapter—are: the *Baltimore Afro-American;* the *Burlington* [N.C.] Times-*News;* the *Greensboro* [N.C.] *Daily News* and the *Greensboro Daily News and Record* (Sunday ed.); the *Miami Herald; The New York Times;* and the *Washington Post;* and the *Norfolk* [Va.] *Virginian-Pilot.*

Appendix:
Professional Publications of
Charles R. Drew

The authors' names appear in order of seniority.

Drew, C. R. and Sloan, L. W. "Anhydremia in Appendicitis." *Surgical Clinics of North America* 19 (Apr., 1939): 295–306.

Scudder, J., Drew, C. R., Corcoran, D. R., and Bull, D. C. "Studies in Blood Preservation." *Journal of the American Medical Association* 112 (June 3, 1939): 2263–71.

Scudder, J., Smith, M. E., and Drew, C. R. "Plasma Potassium Content of Cardiac Blood at Death." *American Journal of Physiology* 126 (June, 1939): 337–40.

Drew, C. R., Edsall, K., and Scudder, J. "Studies in Blood Preservation: Fate of Cellular Elements in Relation to Potassium Diffusion." *Journal of Laboratory and Clinical Medicine* 25 (Dec., 1939): 240–45.

Drew, C. R., Scudder, J., and Papps, J. "Controlled Fluid Therapy, with Hematocrit, Specific Gravity, and Plasma Protein Determination." *Surgery, Gynecology, and Obstetrics* 70 (May, 1940): 859–67.

Smith, M. E., Tuthill, E., Drew, C. R., and Scudder, J. "Studies in Blood Preservation: Some Effects of Carbon Dioxide." *Journal of Biological Chemistry* 133, (Apr., 1940): 499–501.

Scudder, J., Corcoran, D. R., and Drew, C. R. "Studies in Blood Preservation: Serum Potassium of Cadaver Blood." *Surgery, Gynecology, and Obstetrics* 70 (1940): 48–50.

Bull, D. C., and Drew, C. R. "Symposium on Fluid and Electrolyte Needs of Surgical Patient: Preservation of Blood." *Annals of Surgery* 112 (1940): 498–501.

Scudder, J., Bishop, K., and Drew, C. R. "Studies in Blood Preservation:

Shape of the Container." *Journal of the American Medical Association* 115 (July 27, 1940): 290.

Scudder, J., Drew, C. R., and Damon, V. G. "Studies in Preservation of Placental Blood." *American Journal of Obstetrics and Gynecology* 40 (Sept., 1940): 461–63.

Drew, C. R., Contributor to Scudder, J. *Shock—Blood Studies as a Guide to Therapy.* Philadelphia: J.B. Lippincott, 1940.

Scudder, J., Drew, C. R., Tuthill, E., and Smith, M. E. "Newer Knowledge of Blood Transfusions." *Bulletin of the New York Academy of Medicine* 17 (May, 1941): 373–98.

Drew, C. R., and Scudder, J. "Studies in Blood Preservation: Fate of Cellular Elements and Prothrombin in Citrated Blood." *Journal of Laboratory and Clinical Medicine* 26 (June, 1941): 1473–78.

Drew, C. R., Stetten, D., Rhoads, C. P., and Scudder, J. *Report Concerning the Project for Supplying Blood to England.* New York: Blood Transfusion Improvement Association, 1941.

Scudder, J., Drew, C.R., Tuthill, E., and Smith, M. E. "Newer Knowledge of Blood Transfusions." *Bulletin of the New York Academy of Medicine* 17 (1941): 373–398.

Drew, C. R. "Early Recognition and Treatment of Shock," *Anesthesiology* 3 (Mar., 1942): 176–94.

Drew, C. R. "Role of Soviet Investigators in Development of the Blood Bank." *American Review of Soviet Medicine* 1 (Apr., 1944): 360–69.

Malloy, H. R., Jason, R. S., and Drew, C. R. "Role of Lymphoid Hyperplasia in Acute Appendicitis." *American Journal of Surgery* 67 (Jan., 1945): 81–86.

Burton, A. F., and Drew, C. R. "The Clinical Use of a New Protein Preparation." *Journal of The National Medical Association* 41 (Mar., 1949): 74.

Ford, J. R., and Drew, C. R. "Appendicitis in the American Negro." *American Journal of Surgery* 80 (Sept., 1950): 341–44 (published posthumously).

White, J. E., and Drew, C. R. "Perforating Gunshot Wounds of the Abdomen." *Journal of The National Medical Association* 43 (1951): 14–19 (published posthumously).

Index

127

A Note on the Author

Charles E. Wynes is a professor of history at the University of Georgia, Athens, Georgia. During the course of his long career as a specialist in black history, he has authored numerous articles and edited several books, namely, *Southern Sketches from Virginia, 1881–1901, The Negro in the South since 1865,* and *Forgotten Voices: Dissenting Southerners in an Age of Conformity.* In addition Professor Wynes is the author of *Race Relations in Virginia, 1870–1902* (1961) and co-author of *A History of Georgia* (1977).

BOOKS IN THE SERIES BLACKS IN THE NEW WORLD

Black Leaders of the Nineteenth Century
Edited by Leon Litwack and August Meier

Charles Richard Drew: the Man and the Myth
Charles E. Wynes

Reprint Editions
King: A Biography
David Levering Lewis Second Edition

The Death and Life of Malcolm X
Peter Goldman Second Edition

Race Relations in the Urban South, 1865–1890
Howard N. Rabinowitz, with a Foreword by C. Vann Woodward

Race Riot at East St. Louis, July 2, 1917
Elliott Rudwick

W. E. B. Du Bois: Voice of the Black Protest Movement
Elliott Rudwick

The Negro's Civil War: How American Negroes Felt and Acted during the
War for the Union
James M. McPherson

Lincoln and Black Freedom: A Study in Presidential Leadership
LaWanda Cox

Slavery and Freedom in the Age of the American Revolution
Edited by Ira Berlin and Ronald Hoffman